WORKING THE DIRT

NEWSOUTH BOOKS
Montgomery

WORKING THE DIRT

An Anthology of Southern Poets

Edited and with a Preface by

Jennifer Horne

NewSouth Books
P.O. Box 1588
Montgomery, AL 36102

Library of Congress Cataloging-in-Publication Data

ISBN 1-58838-131-5

Design by Randall Williams
Printed in the United States of America

"Now you go out there, like in the summertime, and you work it [the soil]. You'll bring the moisture up. But when you stop work, the ground will bake and it will get dry. Everyone wondered why we could have vegetables and flowers. It was because we kept working it. If you stop working your garden, you've just lost out." —Sadie Johnson of Alabama, in *African-American Gardens and Yards in the Rural South,* by Richard Westmacott

Contents

III. AS FOR MAN

IV. STRONG WOMEN

IV. FRUITS AND VEGETABLES

VI. Yards and Gardens

PREFACE

This book began in the simplest way possible: with the idea that, as someone who enjoys both gardening and poetry, I would myself like to read a book of gardening poems. I found that a few such books do exist—but none reflected the specific history and climate of the South, where I grew up and continue to live. From there it was another step to decide that I might be the person to compile such a book, and as I went along, reading my favorite Southern poets and discovering new ones, I developed the notion that perhaps the South had a distinctive body of poems related to gardening.

A fortuitous conversation with the editor Randall Williams, long before he accepted this book for publication, led me to include poems about farming as well. (Randall will remind you that he has actually picked cotton.) We were sitting next to one another at a banquet for Birmingham-Southern's Writing Today conference and comparing notes about our current projects. I told him about my book of Southern gardening poems and complained, "But I keep finding all these *farming* poems, and I don't know what to do with them!" Our subsequent conversation made me think about what is actually the close relationship between gardening and farming in the South and to observe that, in my experience, most Southerners are just one generation—or less—removed from the farm. I'm not sure that's true about other regions of the country. Many of the poems in this book have as their subject *memory*: remembering a grandparent whose farm the speaker visited as a child, such as James Applewhite's "My Grandfather's Funeral" or "Morning Glory," by Richard Jackson, revisiting the family homeplace with its sweet, or bitter, memories—as in Henry Taylor's "Harvest" and Emily Hiestand's "Planting in Tuscaloosa," and perhaps most of all acknowledging the metaphorical dirt under one's fingernails, as in Fred Chappell's "My Grandmother Washes Her Feet." In a variant on the biblical "dust to dust," we have "dirt to dirt"—dirt on our hands, dirt on our feet; we come from dirt, and we never quite leave it behind.

A couple of books have made an impression on me and no doubt had an influence on this book. The first is *All God's Dangers: The Life of Nate Shaw*, by Theodore Rosengarten. It tells the story of Ned Cobb, called Nate Shaw in the book, a black Alabama cotton farmer who joined a sharecroppers union in the 1930s and later ended up in prison, partly as a result of refusing to name other union members, and it helped me to understand the history of those fields I'd drive by on weekend rambles. The other I came to relatively late, after reading an article by Mindy Wilson on Walker Evans's photos of Hale County sharecroppers in *Let Us Now Praise Famous Men* in the magazine I was working for at the time, *Alabama Heritage*. That book, by James Agee, with photos by Evans, stunned me with its lyricism and its word pictures. I studied Evans's photos like family portraits, and one day, in the way unusual things sometimes just happened at *Alabama Heritage*, one of the Burroughs boys from one of those pictures walked in the door of the nineteenth-century house where we had our offices. Grown now, of course, but recognizable. He wanted some extra copies of the issue to give to his family.

Also here in Tuscaloosa, I found my way to the University of Alabama Arboretum, which sounds as though it might be just trees but is in fact a busy and fertile nexus of gardening activity run by its horticulturist, Mary Jo Modica. I will be forever grateful to Mary Jo for taking in an eager newcomer and teaching her about starting seedlings, planning and planting a bed, and growing sweet-flavored golden tomatoes. My poem in this book takes place at the arboretum and is dedicated to her son, Michael.

I would recommend to anyone interested in Southern gardening and its cultural history the writings of Felder Rushing, whose book *Passalong Plants* brought to life for me a whole way of gardening that has little to do with chain home improvement stores and lots to do with making human connections over the garden fence.

These are a few of the main influences, the currents that flowed together to help me conceptualize this book.

This book is made up of six sections that take the reader, in one way of reading, through an impressionistic history of Southern agriculture: from farmers to migrants, and the men and women who worked those farms, to the pleasures of summer fruits and vegetables and their winter cousins—jars of put-up peaches, pickles, preserves, and on to the present, to our Southern yards and gardens, some with ornamentals only but many with that little patch for the kitchen—early on, some radishes and lettuces, later tomatoes, peppers, squash. Maybe the lettuces now are arugula and mâche, the peppers hot, the patch punctuated with Thai basil, Italian flat-leaf parsley, lemon thyme. But the urge is the same: to get out there in the sun on your knees and get your hands dirty, to feel the life of a plant in your fingers and to nourish it and watch over it and then enjoy its produce.

So this book can be read straight through as a kind of a novel in poems about planting in the South. It can also be read section by section, to soak oneself in a single subject. Compiling the section titled "Strong Women," I thought about both my grandmothers, one a hard-working seamstress and store clerk who did not have time to grow much but who cooked heaping Sunday dinners for her eight children and then for all us grandchildren and from whom I learned what vegetables—purple-hull peas, corn on the cob, new potatoes, cabbage, okra, lima beans, string beans—were supposed to taste like;

the other a Southern gentlewoman who fooled a visiting neighbor child into liking squash by calling it "squizzard" and never had anything to do with fields in her life until a late second marriage took her to southern California, where she and her husband delighted in going with the other senior citizens to the tomato fields, after they'd been picked, to glean what bounty still remained.

I also thought of my mother, to whom I owe more than I can ever say, in the realms of both gardening and poetry. She was the daughter chosen to work with her father in World War II on his victory garden and who never lost her love of plants, beginning her planning for the summer in winter, by the fire, with catalogues, diagrams, lists ("Perhaps some ajuga under the fountain . . .). Visits to Hocott's Garden Center on Kavanaugh Boulevard in Little Rock were a regular part of my growing up, a frequent after-school errand, and I have forever in my sense memory that rich, humid, earthy smell that hit your nostrils as you entered, and the sound of water trickling from many fountains. On vacation, my mother would insist on visiting Bellingrath Gardens or stopping at a roadside stand for fresh produce on the way home. "How are you selling your peaches?" she'd ask, meaning how much are they. In spring we picked jonquils from a field ablaze with thousands of them in a little community out Highway 10 from Little Rock. I didn't realize until she was gone how much I had counted on her to remember the names of things: jonquil, hyacinth, hydrangea, jasmine—and a part of this book comes from wanting to learn those things by heart.

Another part comes from my father's stories of picking peaches as a child, of how the fuzz made his skin itch, how he hated it. He wears suits now instead of overalls and prefers golf courses to gardens, but his stories awakened in me a curiosity about that other life, the one just outside of Little Rock that came to town every weekend with the farmer's market and wore overalls and print dresses and said "ma'am" a lot. Just married at 22 and visiting the downtown farmer's market on my lunch hour, I stopped at one truck and the hefty man selling tomatoes said "Hey girl, how can I help you?" I began to tell him what I wanted, but before I could he corrected himself, catching sight of my wedding ring: "You ain't a girl, you're a woman—now what do you need?" Flipping through my well-worn *Joy of Cooking* the other day, I happened across a clipping, undated, from the old *Arkansas Gazette*. It was a poem I'd cut out years ago, by Marcia Camp of Little Rock and titled "Farmer's Market." To sum up, she writes that, however wonderful, it isn't the vegetables and fruits we come to farmer's markets for; rather, "We're here to see hardy faces (our parents and / grandparents with different features) . . . / For we need to hear the vernacular of hill, / prairie and delta in / words carefully weeded from our city talk, / have our nostrils sting from manure on boots." We need to know, she writes, "that we did not dream childhood."

As farms get larger and more corporate, and we get more generations removed from the small hill and delta farms of our forebears, I believe we still need and seek that connection. Across the country, at the same time the work week gets longer, vacations get shorter, and more and more people work in sterile offices in sealed buildings, gardening is still one of the fastest-growing pursuits in the country. Even in the heat of August, as Jim Mersmann writes in "Letting the Garden Go," we are thinking about next year, ordering catalogues, ready despite the frustrations to work the dirt all over again.

I.
THE FARM

FRED CHAPPELL

The Farm

The hay, the men, are roaring on the hill, July
Muzzy and itchy in the field, broad sunlight
Holds in its throat the tractor's drone, dark bees
Like thumbs in the white cut bolls of clover.
Summer in the fields, unsparing fountain
Of heat and raw savor. Men redden and boil
With sweat, torsos flash, talk, and the laughing
Jet up cool, single cool sound in saffron air,
Air like a yellow cloak. The land is open,
At the mercy of the sky, the trembling sun and sky.
One cloud drives east. Cattle plunder the brackish pools,
Drop awkward shadows while black flies fumble on their skins;
Ruminate; and observe the hour with incurious eye.

The mouths of the men are open, dark medals dangling.
They gulp fierce breath. If a breeze lift the field, skins cloy
With dust. Grin and gouge; neck muscles first tire;
Exhaustion laps the bodies, the mouths are desperately open.
The woman brings water, clear jar echoing
Rings of light fluttering on her apron. Wagon heaped,
   bronze-green
Shaggy hay like a skirt about it, halts then sways
Gingerly to the barn. Bronze-green tongues of it leap
To the sill; harry it in and the loft is bulging, loft
Surfeited beneath the tin roof of fire. Mouse-gray

Pigeons march, dipping beaks like shards of flower pots.

. . . And the hill bared for the blackbirds, swoop in a burst net,
Scattered like pepper specks; men, shouts of flesh, gone
Home, to the wash basins, to tables glowing
With victual. Slow dark enfolds them all, mountains
Empurple and encroach.
                              Hay away, tobacco then and
Corn as the ground dies and cools and barns huddle
In weird light, bats in the gray dusk like pendulums.
Goldenrod indolent, blue moonlets of chickory, Queen
Anne's lace precise as the first stars of frost. Ponds
Grimace and show their teeth under a wind slicing southeast.

The land is puckered and now not open.

Trees thrash, noble and naked wrestlers. Clouds
Mass in the high winds. Birds go away, the shining
Ones, but quail and bobwhite keep the earth. Grass
Graying, thistleweed spending its baubles, frost drives
Deep into rind and pith. The brittle season. Crash crash
Of leaves in seemly groves; late-sweet austerity; blue grapes;

Last glimmer of crickets.

Then winter in the hearth, snaps and snaps
Like cap-pistols the sizzling oak joint and the smoke
Goes bare under the sky. The grandfather snorts
And nods and the chessboard idles while whiskey
Nudges his elbow. All rooms grow smaller, the house
Tightens and the roof howls. Creak creak
The timbers mutter. Ice like cheesecloth on still waters.

Glass needles in the ground. Clear rime. Rattles; clinks;

Stupor of cold wide stars.

And winter in the constricted fields, wind from dead
North mauling the cattle together, furrows hides
Red and white, sifts into the creases fine snow
Like moss; they moan at the gates, turning the helpless eye.
Barns let the blow in, spaces between boards
Crusted slick, sleet piddles the foil-like roofs.
The sky a single gray smear and beneath it flesh
Pinches and rasps, reluctant in unyielding skin . . .

Sun, blind on the first deep snow, every edge
Departs nature, revealing its truthful contour;
Nothing is stark now. The light enlarges and enlarges
Such a fearful blue the head is pained, and burns;
And the body feels evanescent as mist. Sky cloudless,
Birdless, merciless.
                              Night closes over, deep
Crucible; land creeps to star-marge; horizon
Cluttered with light, indifferent emblem of eternity.

Nothing will move but the sauntering wheel of sky

Axis that fixes and orders rolling slowly on a hub of ice.

The houses burrow deeper and deeper.

The world, locked bone.

LILY PETER

Delta Rain

(from "The Cypress Bayou")

Across the brown delta loam
the thin green cotton rows run to woods along the bayou,
where the bullfrogs bellow among the cypress knees
in the cool dimness of the cloudy May afternoon.
A finger of lightning reaches down to the treetops
where the south wind whips up the leaves like ivory lace
against the hyacinthine blue of the rain clouds,
and the rain follows with its silver shadow.
The treetoads call to each other from the China trees;
a mockingbird trills from its nesting place in the cedars.
In the rain-sweet air drifts the fragrance of roadside honeysuckle.

The May rain lasts but an hour, yet this remembrance
will refresh a scorched season of August drought.

Walter McDonald

Starting a Pasture

This far out in the country no one is talking,
no rescue squads row by in boats to prairie land
so dry the Ogallala water table drops
three feet every year. The digger rams down
through dirt no plow has turned. In the heat
I let my mind run wild. For days I've thought
the world is ending, the red oaks turning red
again, the last geese there could be
stampeding from the north, surviving
to show us the only hope, the tips of their
arrow formations pointing the way. So many birds,
if the world doesn't end this will be for Canada
the year of the locust. I shake my head
at my schemes, and sweat flies: cattle
on cottónland. The market for beef
is weak, the need for cotton constant.
I might as well raise goats and sheep as cows,
or trap for bounty the wolves and coyotes
that claim my fields at night. I might as well
rent a steam shovel and dig a lake deep as an ark,
empty my last irrigation well to fill it green enough
for geese on the flyway both seasons. I could
raise trout and channel cat, horses and bees
like the pastures of heaven, gazelles and impala

imported from other deserts, two of each kind
of animals in a dying world.

                    Sun going down,
the last hole dug, the last post dropped
and tamped tight enough to hold three strands of wire,
I toss the digger in the pickup between bales
of barbed wire ready for stringing, the calves
I bought last week already overdue, the feedbill
mounting. My father used to say a man could lift
a bull if he'd practice on a calf each day.
Pulling my gloves back on, I lift the first bale
out and nail the end, uncoil the wire and nail it
tight on the posts. And as it turns dark
I go on stretching and nailing until I don't care
how many neighbors drive by with their lights on,
honking, sticking their heads out the windows and laughing.

A. R. AMMONS

Silver

I thought Silver must have snaked logs
when young:
she couldn't stand to have the line brush her lower hind leg:
in blinded halter she couldn't tell what had loosened behind her
and was coming
as downhill
to rush into her crippling her to the ground:

and when she almost went to sleep, me dreaming at the slow plow,
I would
at dream's end turning over the mind to a new chapter
let the line drop and touch her leg
and she would
bring the plow out of the ground with speed but wisely
fall soon again into the slow requirements of our dreams:
how we turned at the ends of rows without sense to new furrows
and went back
flicked by
cornblades and hearing the circling in
the cornblades of horseflies in pursuit:

I hitch up early, the raw spot on Silver's shoulder
sore to the collar,
get a wrench and change the plow's bull-tongue for a sweep,
and go out, wrench in my hip pocket for later adjustments,

                down the ditch-path
by the white bloomed briars, wet crabgrass, cattails,
                and rusting ferns,
riding the plow handles down,
                keeping the sweep's point from the ground,
the smooth bar under the plow gliding,
the traces loose, the raw spot wearing its soreness out
in the gentle movement to the fields:

                when snake-bitten in the spring pasture grass
Silver came up to the gate and stood head-down enchanted
                in her fate
I found her sorrowful eyes by accident and knew:
nevertheless the doctor could not keep her from all
the consequences, rolls in the sand, the blank extension
                of limbs,
                head thrown back in the dust,
useless unfocusing eyes, belly swollen
wide as I was tall
and I went out in the night and saw her in the solitude
                of her wildness:

but she lived and one day half got up
and looking around at the sober world took me back
                into her eyes
and then got up and walked and plowed again;
mornings her swollen snake-bitten leg wept bright as dew
and dried to streaks of salt leaked white from the hair.

Robert Morgan

Topsoil

Sun's heat collects in leaf crystals
crumbling.
Earth grinds the grain
to dark flour, drifts black flannel
over rock and clay.
Life invests
and draws on.
A lake rises over the world,
heaps of the rotting ocean.
Suns' heat adding
weight
piles on its light
century after century tarnishing
earth's metal.
Traffic of roots
hurrying. Places the raw meat
shows through torn to the quick.
Red clay mirrors.
Black fruit
growing around the earth, deepening
in the autumn
sun drifting down.

The Current

Having once put his hand into the ground,
seeding there what he hopes will outlast him,
a man has made a marriage with his place,
and if he leaves it his flesh will ache to go back.
His hand has given up its birdlife in the air.
It has reached into the dark like a root
and begun to work, quick and mortal in timelessness,
a flickering sap coursing upward into his head
so that he sees the old tribespeople bend
in the sun, digging with sticks, the forest opening
to receive their hills of corn, squash, and beans,
their lodges and graves, and closing again.
He is made their descendant, what they left
in the earth rising into him like a seasonal juice.
And he sees the bearers of his own blood arriving,
the forest burrowing into the earth as they come,
their hands gathering the stones up into walls,
and relaxing, the stones crawling back into the ground
to lie still under the black wheels of machines.
The current flowing to him through the earth
flows past him, and he sees one descended from him,
a young man who has reached into the ground,
his hand held in the dark as by a hand.

Randall Jarrell

A Country Life

A bird that I don't know,
Hunched on his light-pole like a scarecrow,
Looks sideways out into the wheat
The wind waves under the waves of heat.
The field is yellow as egg-bread dough
Except where (just as though they'd let
It live for looks) a locust billows
In leaf-green and shade-violet,
A standing mercy.
The bird calls twice, *"Red clay, red clay"*;
Or else he's saying, "Directly, directly."
If someone came by I could ask,
Around here all of them must know—
And why they live so and die so—
Or why, for once, the lagging heron
Flaps from the little creek's parched cresses
Across the harsh-grassed, gullied meadow
To the black, rowed evergreens below.

They know and they don't know.
To ask, a man must be a stranger—
And asking, much more answering, is dangerous;
Asked about it, who would not repent
Of all he ever did and never meant,
And think a life and its distresses,

Its random, clutched-for, homefelt blisses,
The circumstances of an accident?
The farthest farmer in a field,
A gaunt plant grown, for seed, by farmers,
Has felt a longing, lorn urbanity
Jailed in his breast; and just as I,
Has grunted, in his old perplexity,
A standing plea.

From the tar of the blazing square
The eyes shift, in their taciturn
And unavowing, unavailing sorrow.
Yet the intonation of a name confesses
Some secrets that they never meant
To let out to a soul; and what words would not dim
The bowed and weathered heads above the denim
Or the once-too-often-washed wash dresses?

They are subdued to their own element.
One day
The red, clay face
Is lowered to the naked clay;
After some words, the body is forsaken. . . .
The shadows lengthen, and a dreaming hope
Breathes, from the vague mound, *Life*;
From the grove under the spire
Stars shine, and a wandering light
Is kindled for the mourner, man.
The angel kneeling with the wreath
Sees, in the moonlight, graves.

HENRY TAYLOR

Harvest

Every year in late July I come back to where I was raised,
      to mosey and browse through old farm buildings,
      over fields that seem never to change,

rummaging through a life I can no longer lead
      and still cannot leave behind, looking for relics
      which might spring back to that life at my touch.

Today, among thistles and ragweed, I stumble on
      a discarded combine—the old kind we pulled
      with a tractor to cut and thresh barley and wheat.

Now it lies listing into the side of this hill
      like a stone or an uprooted stump, harboring snakes
      and wasps, rusting slowly into the briars.

Still, I climb to the seat, wondering whether it will
      hold me, fumbling for pedals and levers
      I used to know by heart. Above my head,

the grain-pipe forks down to the bag-clamps,
      and a wad of tie-strings, gone weedy and rotten,
      still hangs by my right hand. As I touch these things,

this machine I once knew by many unprintable names

moves out through barley in late July, and the stalks
fall to the knife as the paddle-reel sweeps them in.

On wide canvas belts, cut grain rides into the dark
insides of the combine, where frantic shakers and screens
break the grain loose from the stalks and the chaff;

almost invisible, small spines from the grain-heads
pour out through holes in the metal, billowing
into a cloud that moves with us over the hills,

engulfing me, the machine, the tractor and driver,
as we work in a spiral to the center of the field,
rolling back through the years in a dust cloud.

The spines stick to my skin, work into my pores,
my bloodstream, and finally blaze into my head
like a miniature cactus of hatred for all grain,

for flour and cereal and bread, for mildewed surplus
swelling in midwestern silos. Never again,
I thought once, as I rode out the cloud until sundown,

never again. I climb down and walk out through the thistles,
still breathing fifteen-year-old barley. The years
in the cloud drift back to me. Metal rusts into the hill.

Barley-dust pricks at my brain, and I am home.

Tom Dent

Mississippi Mornings

(for John Buffington)

early early early
before the eternal basketball game
John meeting & greeting the peoples
getting together the latest
proposal
listening to Staple Singers
   dark woods in the house where Feather
lived & the picture of lean
Mississippi girl with hoe staring
somewhere the groan of tractor
chickens, the country green earth
smell memory of last night's gin
folly burned out by the new sun

soon everything moving & the
hustle is on
toward busy new
early early

Shelter

Thin, racing, rain-clouds came down from the North
So low they touched the earth's green thirsting breast;
Ahead of them two silent crows winged South
Toward a pine grove and their hidden nest.

Approaching clouds, the color of cane-juice,
Fetched winds that made the cornblades tremble some;
And beech limbs in the valley swinging loose
Were whispering that rain had finally come.

Then, everywhere about, each greening shoot
Turned its leaflips in prayer toward the skies;
A kildee family rose in wild dispute,
Climbing the stairs of wind with startling cries.

My mule and I ran for a rockcliff roof
And got there dripping wet like arms of trees;
Thankful, we rested in a room rain-proof
And through wind-windows watched rejoicing leaves.

Deep in the white slabs of the welcomed rain
We watched our thirsting corn drink with a will;
We watched stalks bow in thanks and rise again—
Corn drinking rain is something beautiful!

We rested patiently in our dry room
Away from storm and wet wind-touseled weeds;
We smelled clean fragrance of wild phlox in bloom
And watched the lace ferns' dripping silver beads.

My mule with sparkling eyes and tight-drawn lips
Shook raindrops from his ears and closecropped mane
While he dreamed of the rain-washed clover-tips
And tender sweetblades of the growing cane.

My dreams were for the future, I could see
My autumn cornfields with the stubble dead;
I could not let the winter come on me,
Without corn for my cattle and my bread.

I dreamed of corn enough to fill my bin,
Straight rows of perfect grains so smooth and white,
Of summer's ending, winter's setting in,
Of frozen fields frost-glistening in moonlight.

I could not live through summer helter-skelter
And like the grasshopper beg winter bread;
My bin must be security's safe shelter
When all my fertile fields are winter-dead.

James Still

Heritage

I shall not leave these prisoning hills
Though they topple their barren heads to level earth
And the forests slide uprooted out of the sky.
Though the waters of Troublesome, of Trace Fork,
Of Sand Lick rise in a single body to glean the valleys,
To drown lush pennyroyal, to unravel rail fences;
Though the sun-ball breaks into ridges into dust
And burns its strength into the blistered rock
I cannot leave. I cannot go away.

Being of these hills, being one with the fox
Stealing into the shadows, one with the new-born foal,
The lumbering ox drawing green beech logs to mill,
One with the destined feet of man climbing and descending,
And one with death rising to bloom again, I cannot go.
Being of these hills I cannot pass beyond.

R. T. SMITH

Reaper

So I went out to sling
milkweed down that
tomatoes might grow
by the fence and
all afternoon the handle
got salty in
blistering palms,
the cows lowed, strangers
waved to see me
mowing so, vulnerable
to sun, back-naked,
burned, rhythmic,
entranced by
falling green, the
slim timber of
rabbit tobacco and
that silence close
behind the scythe
sweep.

JIM WAYNE MILLER

Hanging Burley

I'm straddling the top tier, my wet shirt clinging;
under this hot tin roof sweat balls and rolls.
Smothered in gummy green, my seared eyes stinging,
I'm hanging burley tobacco on peeled tier poles.
A funeral mood below me on the ground:
a blank-faced filing past the loaded sled;
a coming with a solemn, swishing sound;
tobacco borne as if it were the dead.
Even the children, shadowed by our grief,
hang broken leaves and ape the studied pace.
—Let burley come, and save each frog-eyed leaf,
till every wilted stick is hung in place,
till gazing on the naked, empty field,
we see, row after row, your death revealed.

Shelby Stephenson

Tobacco Days

The rows almost ridge themselves, shaping the year again
towards seasons that let the dust of sandlugs
fall into yesterdays lost in failed crops, quick dreams.

———————

I lay on the warm ground of the Mayo barn at four in the morning
hoping Brother would oversleep.
The flatbed trailer bounded across the ditch, the Farmall Cub
    droned.
"Morning, boys," I climbed the tierpoles.
Taking the top, I handed down four sticks at a time to Lee to
Paul who packed the trailer. From my perch I
stirred the sun through airholes under the eaves.
The barn emptied, we walked through dew to breakfast.
Dreams drifted awkwardly, Brother's Big Man chew
rolling over in sand-dust.

———————

The tobacco greens for the farmer who dives into the dirt,
renewed in the smell of warehouses,
golden leaves in the lightholes bringing the legged sunlight in.
Dew in dust, a musk in mist,
the tobacco tips one more time on the prime,

a sea of blooms
bobbing in ninetyfive degree wisps of heat,
adhesive tape slipping over blisters.

My bare feet burn on the ground and I shuffle
toes into dirt for moisture, inching stalk by stalk
down endless rows in the ten-acre field where short rows
fade into plumbushes and shade.

The mules on the drags
relax through the hot, climbing
July days, the frying dust, and you wonder if you'll ever
get the gum off your hands.

The Farmer

In the still-blistering late afternoon,
like currying a horse the rake
circled the meadow, the cut grass ridging
behind it. This summer, if the weather held,
he'd risk a second harvest after years
of reinvesting, leaving fallow.
These fields were why he farmed—
he walked the fenceline like a man in love.
The animals were merely what he needed: cattle
and pigs; chickens for a while; a drayhorse,
saddle horses he was paid to pasture—
an endless stupid round
of animals, one of them always hungry, sick, lost,
calving or farrowing, or waiting slaughter.

When the field began dissolving in the dusk,
he carried feed down to the knoll,
its clump of pines, gate, trough, lick, chute
and two gray hives; leaned into the Jersey's side
as the galvanized bucket filled with milk;
released the cow and turned to the bees.
He'd taken honey before without protection.
This time, they could smell something
in his sweat—fatigue? impatience,
although he was a stubborn, patient man?

Suddenly, like flame, they were swarming over him.
He rolled in the dirt, manure and stiff hoof-prints,
started back up the path, rolled in the fresh hay—
refused to run, which would have pumped
the venom through him faster—passed the oaks
at the yard's edge, rolled in the yard, reached
the kitchen, and when he tore off his clothes
crushed bees dropped from him like scabs.

For a week he lay in the darkened bedroom.
The doctor stopped by twice a day—
the hundred stings "enough to kill an ox,
enough to kill a younger man." What saved him
were the years of smaller doses—
like minor disappointments,
instructive poison, something he could use.

R. H. W. Dillard

The Mullins Farm

The sun through the window
Is as warm as the smell of salt,
Of hams, the hum of bees
Where the smoke bellows lie
On the table by the netting,
The hat and the gloves.

My uncle hands you a turtle's heart,
Beating, beating in your open hand.
His head still hooked on the broom,
The hollow of his bones on the ground,
And his parts laid out by the fire,
The kettle made ready for soup.

The high horse, Mack, dappled white,
And the brown, too, slow and full,
The hill that falls off from the barn
Where the corn is husked in the dark,
And the hogs hanging to be split,
Filled with apples and corn and sweet slop.

By the branch out back and the small bridge,
In the damp concrete walls, the milk
Sits in spring water, and the squares
Of pressed butter, each with its bouquet

Of spring flowers, and on the bank,
An occasional frog or small snake.

The horseshoes must be bent on hot coals,
Red and white as new flowers, sprinkled
On the ground around the anvil, inviting
To your hand which must never touch,
And the shadows of the waiting horses,
The hot hammers, the hard men.

And the red hen in your arms is soft
And warm as the smell of feathers,
As the afternoon, while a small hawk
Watches from a crooked pine, watches
My grandfather in his clean tan clothes
Load his shotgun in the porch's shade.

And my grandmother rings the wood stove,
Takes the biscuits from the high warmer,
Calls her daughters to set the table,
And feeds the large family with squirrel
And green beans, squash and mashed potatoes
As a brace of dead crows hang from the fence.

The afternoon is unending and clear
As the branches in front of and behind
The white house, as you climb the hill
To the barn, smell the stacked hay,
Touch the smooth wood of the stalls,
And see the sun powdered by barn dust.

My grandfather has cut a log of green wood
And set it up in the fireplace
With dry props to light as the evening
Comes on, and you may sit in the dim room
With the shadows wrinkling your face,
Hear the fire living in the light's slow leak.

The hounds are asleep on the front porch,
Their flat brown ears and sharp ribs,
While the cats climb to eat on a fence post,
And the oaks rattle acorns in the grass
And on the tin roof of the porch,
And the corn stalks crack in the air.

MARION MONTGOMERY

Dry Lightning

"If . . . if it don't rain soon," he said
And kicked his foot in the dust to finish out the threat.
The grey puffs settled on his shoes,
Cracked like the bottom where corn sagged.

"If it don't rain soon . . ."
A hot breeze rustled in the field,
On beyond the line of hills dry lightning raised a non-
     committal glow.
"If it don't rain . . ."
The lightning teased again.

Edsel Ford

Because He Turned His Back

A man can turn his back upon a farm
And let a city street replace his meadow,
And he can lend to other tasks the arm
Which shook gooseberries from the deepest shadow,
And he can punch a clock with that same hand
Which swung a sickle through bright clouds of fescue.
But when his heart beneath cement and sand
Hardens, who can then effect his rescue?
There is a supermarket in his grove,
A filling station where he milked the cows.
The little apple orchard which he strove
So hard to nurture has been sheared to house
A parking lot; and there's a go-kart track
In his front yard—because he turned his back.

James Whitehead

Delta Farmer in a Wet Summer

Last summer was hot and dry, a better time—
Two cuttings at the dock and two knocked up
In the fields, and a crop to fill the wagons full.
There were prime steaks and politics at night—
Gin to nine and bourbon after that.
By God, we raised some handsome bales and hell,
Then went to New Orleans as usual.

But now it rains too long, too little sun
To stop the rot. Rain beats down on the roof
At night and gives sad dreams—black bolls—
And the Thunderbird will have to go. You can smell
It on the evenings, like the smell of a filthy
Bed, or wasted borrowed money, the stink
Of a bloated dog when finally the water's down.

. . . in California they say it's dry.
They irrigate consistently, don't count
The weather in when going to the bank,
And that's damned smart, except they've got no woods
Or sloughs to crowd the fields, and dogs get killed
But rarely drown—and I think our bitch, stretched hide
And stench, contains the element of chance a Christian needs.

II.
Moving On, Digging In

Robert Penn Warren

Kentucky Mountain Farm

I. REBUKE OF THE ROCKS

Now on you is the hungry equinox,
O little stubborn people of the hill,
The season of the obscene moon whose pull
Disturbs the sod, the rabbit, the lank fox,
Moving the waters, the boar's dull blood,
And the acrid sap of the ironwood.

But breed no tender thing among the rocks.
Rocks are too old, under the mad moon,
Renouncing passion by the strength that locks
The eternal agony of fire in stone.

The quit yourselves as stone, and cease
To break the weary stubble-field for seed;
Let not the naked cattle bear increase,
Let barley wither and the bright milk-weed.
Instruct the heart, lean men, of a rocky place
That even the little flesh and fevered bone
May keep the sweet sterility of stone.

II. AT THE HOUR OF THE BREAKING OF THE ROCKS

Beyond the wrack and eucharist of snow
The tortured and reluctant rock again
Receives the sunlight and the tarnished rain.
Such is the hour of sundering, we know,
Who on the hills have seen to stand and pass
Stubbornly the taciturn
Lean men that of all things alone
Were, not as water or the febrile grass,
Figured in kinship to the savage stone.

The hills are weary, the lean men have passed;
The rocks are stricken, and the frost has torn
Away their ridged fundaments at last,
So that the fractured atoms now are borne
Down shifting waters to the tall, profound
Shadow of the absolute deeps,
Wherein the spirit moves and never sleeps
That held the foot among the rocks, that bound
The tired hand upon the stubborn plow,
Knotted the flesh unto the hungry bone,
The red-bud to the charred and broken bough,
And strung the bitter tendons of the stone.

III. HISTORY AMONG THE ROCKS

There are many ways to die
Here among the rocks in any weather:
Wind, down the eastern gap, will lie
Level along the snow, beating the cedar,
And lull the drowsy head that it blows over

To start a crystalline, cold dream forever.

The hound's black paw will print the grass in May,
And sycamores rise down a dark ravine,
Where a creek in flood, sucking the rock and clay,
Will tumble the sycamore, the laurel, away.
Think how a body, naked and lean
And white as the splintered sycamore, would go
Tumbling and turning, hushed in the end,
With hair afloat in waters that gently bend
To ocean where the blind tides flow.

Under the shadow of ripe wheat,
By flat limestone, will coil the copperhead,
Fanged as the sunlight, hearing the reaper's feet.
But there are other ways, the lean men said:
In these autumn orchards once young men lay dead—
Grey coats, blue coats. Young men on the mountainside
Clambered, fought. Heels muddied the rocky spring.
Their reason is hard to guess, remembering
Blood on their black mustaches in moonlight,
Cold musket-barrels glittering with frost.
Their reason is hard to guess and a long time past;
The apple falls, falling in the quiet night.

ROBERT MORGAN

Steep

Driven out from the centers of population,
displaced from villages and crossroads and too poor
to acquire the alluvial bottomlands,
the carbon-dark fields along the creek,

forced back on the rocky slopes above branches,
to the flanks near the headwaters,
pushed to the final mountain wall, I brace
my faculties against falling out of labor

and prop up or stake down every stalk, dig
terraces and drive fences to save what little
topsoil there is from the gullywashers
hitting almost every afternoon up here in summer.

Cow trails babel the steepest knobs, make
by spiral and switchback the sheer peaks
and outcroppings accessible. I plant only root
vegetables, turnips, potatoes, and prehensile creepers.

Too far to carry whole or raw things
into town, I take the trouble only with something
boiled down, distilled, and clear new
ground every three or four years.

I live high on the hogback near
dividing water, I disaffiliate and secede.
I grow ginseng in hollows unlit as the dark
side of the moon, and confederate with moisture and

insular height to bring summit orchards
to bear. I husband the scartissue of erosion.

C. D. Wright

Landlocked, Fallen, Unsung

(in praise of Agee)

Those who went shares, plodded
Through the dust of their life. Like a horse.
A swayback woman would get up
From red dreams, cross an uneven floor
Before the cock on the hood cleared his throat.
In sleep, the man
Hurled another stone at the sun.
The visitor from the North
Pretended not to rouse,
Not watch her
Pull a rag off a hook at the washstand,
Scrub her chest, wipe blood
Between her legs,
Pin her hair up for church
With no mirror.
This was the time
For laying by. He knew. She knew.
He was a shack of a man.
He would cut off his thumbs for her.

Wendell Berry

The Migrants

They depart from what they have failed
to know—old clearings overgrown
with thicket, farmlands mute
under the breath of grazing machines.

Broken from the land, they inherit
a time without history, a future
their fathers did not dream of
and they do not imagine.

Where their fathers took the hill land
the forest returns. Rains usurp the hearths.
The fear of loss dies out
as the sills drift and sink.

GUY OWEN

Deserted Farm

I took a walk through woods and snow
Until I came to a garden row
Gone to sedge, then a gate of boards
Rotting beneath two martin gourds.

A roofless shed, an old turn plow
Said men were here, but not here now.
"Where have they gone?" I asked the pump
Rusting beside the light'ood stump.

Its handle swept toward the sky
(Whatever that might signify);
Its mouth was dry as chimney clay—
And if it knew, it didn't say.

George Scarbrough

Tenantry (Polk County, Tennessee)

Always in transit
we were always temporarily
in exile,
each new place seeming
after a while
and for a while
our home.

Because no matter
how far we traveled
on the edge of strangeness
in a small county,
the earth ran before us
down red clay roads
blurred with summer dust,
banked with winter mud.

It was the measurable,
pleasurable earth
that was home.
Nobody who loved it
could ever be really alien.
Its tough clay, deep loam,
hill rocks, small flowers

were always the signs
of a homecoming.

We wound down through them
to them,
and the house we came to,
whispering with dead hollyhocks
or once in spring
sill-high in daisies,
was unimportant.
Wherever it stood,
it stood on earth,
and the earth welcomed us,
open, gateless,
one place as another.

And each place seemed
after a while
and for a while
our home:
because the county
was only a mansion
kind of dwelling
in which there were many
rooms.
We only moved from one
room to another,
getting acquainted
with the whole house.

And always the earth
was the new floor under us,
the blue pinewoods the walls
rising around us,
the windows the openings
in the blue trees
through which we glimpsed,
always farther on,
sometimes beyond the river,
the real wall of the mountain,
in whose shadow
for a little while
we assumed ourselves safe,
secure and comfortable
as happy animals
in an unvisited lair:

which is why perhaps
no house we ever lived in
stood behind a fence,
no door we ever opened
had a key.

It was beautiful like that.
For a little while.

EDITH L. FRASER

Old Rice-Fields

In all earth's boundless beauty here revealed
There is no lonelier, lovelier, sadder sight
Than flocks of wild geese soaring high in flight
O'er wide, waste waters of an old rice-field.
In royal blueness here the pickerel weed
The spreading, silent, silver lakes enfold;
And yellow lotus blossoms give their gold.
Here grey-brown rice birds that forever feed
On the wild rice that in remaining still
Tells of the days that now are in the past.
Still stands the old rice tower with its floor
Of hand-made bricks, for this was once a mill.
Silver the still lagoons reflect the past,
Mirror of days now gone to come no more.

Ahmos Zu-Bolton II

By the Fifth Generation

it had gotten so bad
that they hated
sugarcane, though
they needed a good crop
to get them thru the winter
(hating that which gave
some prayer to life.

the young ones hated
the most. they blamed the land
for what was not the
land's fault.

they hated the church
for not giving them hope
in this life

o hope, blessed hope
now now now

until they discovered
that their hatred
was hopeless

THAD STEM, JR.

Crisis

An old man leading his jackknife horse
Around the fringe of darkening woods,
Mumbling about the accursed wilt
And wild grass running as ravenously
As a gang of vampires.

The season's terrible, crops are worse,
And idiot papers speak of dark troubles
Somewhere off beyond the horizon.
Trouble is it! By God, they ought
To tangle awhile with downy mildew
That kisses young plants with the lips
Of the devil, himself.

Wonder what's for supper now?
A rasher of fine, lean side meat?
He clucks to his horses excitedly—
Flying sparks from steel on stone
Send fireflies sailing to Settle's Lane.

Scarecrow

Peg-leg actor
Hung with night
Why are you hopping
Largo into my city
Go back
Among your white stalks

Your cross bones
Hold no meat
Your cape
Does not breathe

You are no thing
But the absence of crows

John Beecher

Appalachian Landscape

Sick and scrawny lies the land, denuded
Of forest, sapped of fertility,
Gutted of coal, the integument of life
Flayed utterly from it and bleeding
Its last weak pulse away down washes and gullies.

Scrawny and sick on the stoops of their shacks,
Idle, dejected are the folk of this land.
One sometimes observes them crawling
About their irremediable fields or plodding
Unwashed homewards from their failing mines.

Donald Justice

Sonnet: An Old-Fashioned Devil

> Tu le connais, lecteur, ce monstre délicat . . .
> *Baudelaire*

Who is it snarls our plow lines, wastes our fields,
Unbaits our hooks, and fishes out our streams?
Who leads our hunts to where the good earth yields
To marshlands, and we sink, but no one screams?
Who taught our children where the harlot lives?
They gnaw her nipples and they drain her pap,
Clapping their little hands like primitives
With droll abandon, bouncing on her lap.
Our wives adore him; us he bores to tears.
Who cares if to our dry and yellow grass
He strikes a match or two, then disappears?
It's only the devil on his flop-eared ass—
A beast too delicate to bear him well—
Come plodding by us on his way to hell.

Summer, 1948

John Finlay

A Pastoral of the Primitives

By early June the limbs of the pear tree
Already sag. The weight of its thick fruit
Snaps its joints in just a random breeze,
So rich the womb of meat around the seed!
Sunflowers thrive and blow in deep manure
Where we had kept and fed the fatter bulls
We killed and ate. Noontide is like a god
Who pours himself into the teeming plant
So that we see its essence in white heat.
Only the gross catfish in coffin-vaults
The cows drink water in escape his fire—
They float full-fed on algae and rich scum.
The afternoon expands; the air stays hot.
A bush-hog chews across the pasture just
Below the house, splattered in iron-weed.
White egrets swarm for insects in its wake.
The cows stay for that cooler later time
Before they graze, then eat into the night.
They only stop to throw the head of tongue
Over their backs to kill the biting flies,
Leaving coats of spittle on their hides.
Our sight cannot detect the twilight's end
Or night's degrees. Earth fades in black
Extending upwards from the sunken swamp.
Bullfrogs in sexual heat cry desperately
As a full red moon is rising in the east.

Thomas Rabbitt

The Monday Before Thanksgiving

The swamped sun setting behind the water oaks
Shoots fire across my pasture and my pond,
Past barn and house, and across the road
Into the burnished butterfly pines. Narrow your lids
And your last hopes. All these Alabama trees
Light up like Maine. *Alabama: State of Mind.*
What's wrong is the tragedy of light, the fire
Shot flat through trees in that last flash
We see before the great mad bombs must take us out.
The sun hisses and slips like shit into the swamp.
This morning I promised myself I'd transplant
The roses some fool planted where the cows cross
Coming home. For two years I've waited for his irony
To drop in on me like light from a far off star.
What returns is the realtor carried back by her own
Prismatic sonic booms: dwarf yellow, giant red,
And these, the golden white they call moon sun.
What a card! And I without the courage to see them
For what they are, the names of trash. I prune them
Down to stumps. I dig in. I uproot. I do my best
To spare the fine hairs of the roots, the dark webs
More felt than seen in the small light I have left.
Around me the livestock clamor to be fed. The dogs
Chase pullets up and down the lot. One horse will not
Stop striking his shod forefoot against the metal gate,
The clang insistent as a bell. A pair of turkey hens,

Two bronze phoenixes done up in sunset kerosene,
roost like vultures on the rattling metal gate.
Christmas and Thanksgiving are their cooking names,
Talismans against the cowardice I cannot face.
The horse will not stop striking time against the gate.
From the weedy dam the ducks and geese peer down
And the dogs chase one doomed hen across the pasture,
Through barbed wire and off into the swamp.
Their cries grow faint and the sun goes out like that,
Like danger fading, the air going cooler and cooler.
The roots of the roses do not easily let go; the thorns
Hold back from the night the last of the day's heat.
You dig like that—with ungloved fingers deep
Into the dirt until what you feel is quiet and dark,
Until what you feel is finally cold.

James Dickey

Kudzu

Japan invades. Far Eastern vines
Run from the clay banks they are

Supposed to keep from eroding,
Up telephone poles,
Which rear, half out of leafage,
As though they would shriek,
Like things smothered by their own
Green, mindless, unkillable ghosts.
In Georgia, the legend says
That you must close your windows

At night to keep it out of the house.
The glass is tinged with green, even so,

As the tendrils crawl over the fields.
The night the kudzu has
Your pasture, you sleep like the dead.
Silence has grown Oriental
And you cannot step upon ground:
Your leg plunges somewhere
It should not, it never should be,
Disappears, and waits to be struck

Anywhere between sole and kneecap:
For when the kudzu comes,

The snakes do, and weave themselves
Among its lengthening vines,
Their spade heads resting on leaves,
Growing also, in earthly power
And the huge circumstance of concealment.

One by one the cows stumble in,
Drooling a hot green froth,
And die, seeing the wood of their stalls

Strain to break into leaf.
In your closed house, with the vine

Tapping your window like lightning,
You remember what tactics to use.
In the wrong yellow fog-light of dawn
You herd them in, the hogs,
Head down in their hairy fat,
The meaty troops, to the pasture.
The leaves of the kudzu quake
With the serpents' fear, inside

The meadow ringed with men
Holding sticks, on the country roads.

The hogs disappear in the leaves.
The sound is intense, subhuman,
Nearly human with purposive rage.
There is no terror

Sound from the snakes.
No one can see the desperate, futile
Striking under the leaf heads.
Now and then, the flash of a long

Living vine, a cold belly,
Leaps up, torn apart, then falls

Under the tussling surface.
You have won, and wait for frost,
When, at the merest touch
Of cold, the kudzu turns
Black, withers inward and dies,
Leaving a mass of brown strings
Like the wires of a gigantic switchboard.
You open your windows,

With the lightning restored to the sky
And no leaves rising to bury

You alive inside your frail house,
And you think, in the opened cold,
Of the surface of things and its terrors,
And of the mistaken, mortal
Arrogance of the snakes
As the vines, growing insanely, sent
Great powers into their bodies
And the freedom to strike without warning:

From them, though they killed
Your cattle, such energy also flowed

To you from the knee-high meadow
(It was as though you had
A green sword twined among
The veins of your growing right arm—
Such strength as you would not believe
If you stood alone in a proper
Shaved field among your safe cows—):
Came in through your closed

Leafy windows and almighty sleep
And prospered, till rooted out.

III.
AS FOR MAN

Henry Taylor

Somewhere Along the Way

You lean on a wire fence, looking across
a field of grain with a man you have stopped
to ask for directions. You are not lost.
You stopped here only so you could take a moment
to see whatever this old farmer sees
who crumbles heads of wheat between his palms.

Rust is lifting the red paint from his barn roof,
and earth hardens over the sunken arc
of his mower's iron wheel. All his sons
have grown and moved away, and the old woman
keeps herself in the parlor where the light
is always too weak to make shadows. He sniffs

at the grain in his hand, and cocks an ear
toward a dry tree ringing with cicadas.
There are people dying today, he says,
that never died before. He lifts an arm
and points, saying what you already knew
about the way you are trying to go;

you nod and thank him, and think of going on,
but only after you have stood and listened
a little while longer to the soft click
of the swaying grain heads soon to be cut,
and the low voice, edged with dim prophecy,
that settles down around you like the dust.

Snapshot in the Red Fields

The dirt cakes his boot soles as he steps down from the machine
   idling now in the field the sun slants toward evening and the
     smell
of damp, just-turned earth fills him so that he thinks he will burst
   with it
   he must stop and look, now, before the daylight leaves the
     county,
before the hawk spreads its wings one last time, drops into a row
   and disappears over the grove of trees the machine coughs once,
     a dirty
cloud of diesel plumes into the air he sifts the earth through his
     fingers,
   something he can't touch often enough impossible to explain to
     her,
to anyone, how the fields keep him alive, and at these moments,
     when
   the plow has turned the rows and the earth is open before him
     in its deep
moist iron-rich splendor, he would just as soon dive into it and
     forget
   himself, down, down into its depth, rather than ever lose it or
     know
that the season would not come again.

James Applewhite

My Grandfather's Funeral

I knew the dignity of the words:
"As for man, his days are as grass,
As a flower of the field so he flourisheth:
For the wind passeth, and he is gone"—
But I was not prepared for the beauty
Of the old people coming from the church,
Nor for the suddenness with which our slow
Procession came again in sight of the awakening
Land, as passing white houses, Negroes
In clothes the color of the earth they plowed,
We turned, to see bushes and rusting roofs
Flicker past one way, the stretch of fields
Plowed gray or green with rye flow constant
On the other, away to unchanging pines
Hovering over parallel boles like
Dreams of clouds.
              At the cemetery the people
Surprised me again, walking across
The wave of winter-bleached grass and stones
Toward his grave; grotesques, yet perfect
In their pattern: Wainwright's round head,
His bad shoulder hunched and turning
That hand inward, Luby Paschal's scrubbed
Square face, lips ready to whistle to
A puppy, his wife's delicate ankles

Angling a foot out, Norwood Whitley
Unconsciously rubbing his blue jaw,
Locking his knees as if wearing boots;
The women's dark blue and brocaded black,
Brown stockings on decent legs supporting
Their infirm frames carefully over
The wintry grass that called them down,
Nell Overman moving against the horizon
With round hat and drawn-back shoulders—
Daring to come and show themselves
Above the land, to face the dying
Of William Henry Applewhite,
Whose name was on the central store
He owned no more, who was venerated,
Generous, a tyrant to his family
With his ally, the God of Moses and lightning
(With threat of thunder clouds rising in summer
White and ominous over level fields);
Who kept bright jars of mineral water
On his screened, appled backporch, who prayed
With white hair wispy in the moving air,
Who kept the old way in changing times,
Who killed himself plowing in his garden.
I seemed to see him there, above
The bleached grass in the new spring light,
Bowed to his handplow, bent-kneed, impassive,
Toiling in the sacrament of seasons.

James Seay

Sweetbread and Wine

Zannie Hayes dug in the dark, hard earth
For a dollar and a dime an hour,
Time and a half for overtime,
Until one Sunday when her people were away
His woman asked him if he'd like
              To come in for sweetbread and wine.

Zannie Hayes, though strong from digging in the dark, hard earth,
Trembled all the way across her yard,
Stumbled up the front door steps,
And was on the porch before he finally said
He believed he would
              Come in for sweetbread and wine.

Zannie Hayes who dug in the dark, hard earth
For a dollar and a dime an hour,
Time and a half for overtime,
Now plows his father-in-law's fields
For a dollar and a dime a day,
              Sweetbread and wine for overtime.

Conrad in Twilight

Conrad, Conrad, aren't you old
To sit so late in your mouldy garden?
And I think Conrad knows it well,
Nursing his knees, too rheumy and cold
To warm the wraith of a Forest of Arden.

Neuralgia in the back of his neck,
His lungs filling with such miasma,
His feet dipping in leafage and muck:
Conrad! you've forgotten asthma.

Conrad's house has thick red walls,
The log on Conrad's hearth is blazing,
Slippers and pipe and tea are served,
Butter and toast are meant for pleasing!
Still Conrad's back is not uncurved
And here's an autumn on him, teasing.

Autumn days in our section
Are the most used-up thing on earth
(Or in the waters under the earth)
Having no more color nor predilection
Than cornstalks too wet for the fire,
A ribbon rotting on the byre,
A man's face as weathered as straw
By the summer's flare and winter's flaw.

Guy Owen

My Father's Curse

My father strode in anvil boots
      Across the fields he cursed;
His iron fingers bruised the shoots
      Of green, he stabbed the earth.

My father cursed both sun and rain;
      His sweep cut corn and weed,
And where his fiery plow had lain
      The ruined earth would bleed.

Yet though he raged in bitter brew
      Thick oaths that belled his throat,
God rammed His springing juices through
      And fleshed Himself in fruit.

RICK LOTT

The Gardener

My father cultivated silence
In his cactus garden, spent summer nights
Drinking at a redwood table in the center
Of his thorny geometries,
Watching the night-blooming cereus.
At Easter he travelled to the Dog River
To swim its span and fish the lily pads.

When my father stripped to swim, the roses
In his pale skin astonished the green air.
The day they bloomed, mortars covered a field
Of snow with sudden black blossoms that shook
Their pollen on the soldiers huddled there.
The snow sprouted strange flowers then.

My father always came out of the water
The same man who dove in, unable to douse
The rose of fire in his head.

Now we shovel the ash under,
And pray the lotus blooms in his mouth.

Horace Randall Williams

Laying By

Your crops, old man, are in the hard red
soil of your father's land.
Scooter plow moves through the rows
of Alabama corn; you follow it just
as he did, but each terrace is flatter now.
You have no sons to come hard by, forcing
crumbling furrows to respect the
succession of generations in this labor.

Despite your best efforts, the scrub
oaks have overtaken bottomland
cleared by man and mule forty years ago.
Your grandfather broke it first, but
it lay fallow in his declining years and
you had to work it like new ground.
And now look—

Now dog days are heavy on the
soil. The August heat is parching
the fat ears like meal in a tin
pan in the oven. But you,
you watch the skies, for the rain
comes in the late afternoon.
You are sure of that.

John Allison

Gardening

Independence Day. My father's bean vines
slither farther up their canes every night
to hang black and full knuckled
as the fingers of a thousand field hands.

Deafening electric work and Lucky Strikes killed him,
once, but a rough doctor shook him back.
Now his tomatoes bunch like blue-ribboned hearts.
It's late afternoon and my father
will be in his garden soon.

Two hundred miles away his one son explodes
like fruit dropped dead ripe from the green walls
of a university, and plies his lover who comes
as late as dawn with delicate night birds,
toward the earth.

It's late afternoon and my father
will be in his garden soon.
Hard ground pulls at the roots
of everything he has planted.

Robert Morgan

Sunday Keeping

Every Sunday afternoon in
summer Uncle William drove his
pickup up and down the valley
and to the high nest coves of
the creek to look at others' fields.
He'd stop by the road and, wearing
fresh-ironed khakis, watch chain, dress shoes
with no socks, wade a few rods out
the new plowed rows, avoiding clods
and puddles, and bend to inspect
the young roots and flowers of pole beans,
lift a stray runner to twist on
the fuzzy string, noting the leaf
color and if the blossom had
come before the vine reached halfway
to the wire—a sign of drought
stunting—and if it was late summer
looked for specks of nailhead rust on
the leaves. And if it had been rainy
he reached down to rake the dirt away
to find soreshin on the taproot
and a wheel of white suckers at
the surface. Then he'd slap the bean
dust from his hands and admire
a dark and even stand that thrived

against the luck of weather, or
shake his head at weedy rows and
ragged panels, spit on the posts,
and drive on to another
neighbor's patch to check competition,
observe his neighbor's character,
and maybe feel some victory as
well as kinship, curiosity,
on the day he couldn't work but
couldn't stay away from growing fields.

The Terrapin Maker

For fifty years he followed a mule
Down the furrows of his wife's 40-acre farm,
Forcing each year from the hard red dirt
Several wagonloads of cotton and a crib of corn:
Later he could barely manage a few potatoes.
A yard cleared of Jimson weeds and pusley
And a wife who never believed her mother's absence.
He supported an alcoholic son for thirty years
And brought up a grandson to be killed in a city gang war
And another to be struck by Sunday lightning on the beach.
I saw him last on a borrowed cot,
The cancerous smell of death thick in the room
And mingling with the heavy fragrance of gardenias
Opening white in the front yard.
But I remember him best sitting in a sunny spot
On the middle step of the back porch,
Black wool hat shading his intense blue eyes,
His high topped shoes tightly laced below faded overalls
And snuff spittle drying in the wrinkles of his mouth—
His hands busy with a piece of pine bark
Miraculously becoming a terrapin or a frog
For two little boys approaching in haste
From a mirage of sandy heat.

Wise Enough

So he has made a trellis for her on
The downhill side so that she will have
Roses and, before it rains and at dawn,
The smell of roses. So he is wise enough.

IV.
STRONG WOMEN

JAMES APPLEWHITE

Jonquils

At the ruined homestead in spring,
Where armatures of honeysuckle,
Baskets of weed-wire, sprawl over
Old rows, twine up fruit trees,
Where poison oak thicker than adders chokes about
Stones of a hearth—a broken altar—
The jonquils have risen. Their yellows gather
On sea-colored stems. The frilled bells
Face in all directions, with a scattering of general
Attention toward the sun: now gone, yet source
Of their butter, their gold, this lidded day—
As if sunlight broken in pieces were
Rising from the earth. Like
Bright women abandoned in the wilderness.

RICHARD JACKSON

Morning Glory

She lived in a place where distance
began, testing yellow jackets the way
her grandmother taught her, covering
their hole in a muddy bank with a glass bowl
so they'd fly for a while confused
aiming for a sky too clear to ever reach.

Or she would be looking at skaters,
small insects on the surface of the water
tracing another face over hers,
and beneath, minnows filling her hair
and the pink and blue flowers
that seemed to bloom, reflected there, in
a world she was about to enter or to leave.

Later the smoke would nudge up through
the first shadows, and she would return
downstream to where her family,
there from the north country, camped those few
weeks to harvest apples, migrants for whom
the landscape was an afterthought, like hope.

I say this because she taught me
the first name I remember for a flower,
morning glory, a flowering vine whose roots

begin far from the blossoms, whose heart-shaped leaves
I thought would hold the sun forever,
and because this evening, glimpsing
the face of a girl who stood alone for a moment
amidst the crowd on a street far from that past,
I thought I saw again the underside of those petals.

I had forgotten she believed in a heaven
filled with those flowers. Evenings like this
the sky tries to show you everything
at once. Maybe there is only
one thing in the world we need to heal us,
some first star that claims the whole sky.
Or this flower I had picked in a field
years from here, held in my wallet to spend
when my love would grow so poor,
this morning glory which blooms on the breath
which is our first flowering,
and so returns whatever has been missing,
clinging wherever it will.

SALLIE NIXON

Blue Hosanna

On this last day of June
the fragile morning glories
are giving praise:
Here, they reach
to first light,
stretch their cups
for earliest grace.

I learn from them:
In this still place
I open my own thin blueness,
take deep into myself
the thrust of day.

Nikki Giovanni

A Theory of Pole Beans

(for Ethel and Rice)

that must have been the tail end of the Depression
as well as the depression of coming war
there certainly was segregation and hatred and fear

these small towns and small minded people
trying to bend taller spirits down
were unable to succeed

there couldn't have been too much fun
assuming fun equates with irresponsibility

there was always food to be put on the table
clothes to be washed and ironed
hair to be pressed
gardens to be weeded

and children to talk to and teach
each other to love
and tend to

pole beans are not everyone's favorite
they make you think of pieces of fat back
cornbread

and maybe a piece of fried chicken

they are the staples of things unquestioned
they are broken and boiled

no one would say life handed you
a silver spoon or golden parachute
but you still
met   married
bought a home   reared a family
supported a church   and kept a mighty faith
in your God   and each other

they say love/is a many splendored thing
but maybe that's because we recognize
you loved no matter what the burden
you laughed no matter for the tears
you persevered in your love

and your garden remains in full bloom

David Daniel

December Portrait

(for Stařenka)

There are wet blades of grass bending
over her feet, old feet,
hard and beaten

like veined yellow stones
placed sometime beneath
our blossoming branches.

It is May there, and no traces
of winter cling
to our conversation

which now, I think, is forgotten
or hushed
beneath an inch or two of snow.

Fallen beside us, my grandmother's
gloves are still
curled and brown and strong.

But by this time of year, those weeds she missed
have surely died as she did
despite the interruption of this photograph

and the coming on of evening
to the west
which shadows her face

with grey streaks of poplar
that confuse her
and the landscape

which cracks with my weight
as I walk out, warm and discreet,
into a December evening.

Deborah Pope

Another Valentine

I have come to expect
forsythia stunning
the ragged twigs with random yellow,
the hard spears forking
from the rat's nest of February.
I have come to expect
the south wind treading the lawn
while snow still heaps
like egg shells
in the shade.

Moving up stairs all afternoon
the four o'clock light
holes up in our room,
fingers the careless sheets.
The closets are holding their breath.
In the kitchen stiff cuttings
clatter in a glass jar,
pink clots of quince.
I have had the clippers waiting.

And you, you
sweat easily all morning
raking the winter away,
come in with cool edges,

the smell of raw sun
in your palms,
swing open my heart like a hinge.
I have come to expect it.

Granny Dean

Each spring,
Even when she'd slipped
Past eighty, she scrapped
Her winter drapes
And came out with the green.
Rare the day she wasn't seen
Where wild things bloom,
Time-sprung hands routing daisies
For her small room.

Embroidery

After dark closed its door on a day
as predictable as a loaf of light bread,
with supper dishes, scoured and dried, assuming
their proper stations in the cabinet,
and all homework completed and approved,
we settled into the February night.
Daddy studied prospects for the Dodgers
while, snugly wrapped in flannel and chenille,
Sister and I huddled before the heatrola,
cherishing the reliable warmth it rumbled.

Perched directly under the ceiling light,
Mama firmed an oval of white muslin
across narrow wooden hoops. Squinting,
she threaded skeins of floss through wide-eyed needles,
then fashioned delicate rosy filaments
into graceful petals, coaxed pale green
to glossy leaves, persuaded gentian blue
to flight in the shape of songless birds.

Outside, beyond the wind's blowsy boast,
stars stitched their dazzle into night's black void.
Inside, on a stretched-taut field of cotton
as plainly vanilla as her hours,
Mama, armed with steel and pastel silk,
wrought a garden forever impervious
to late-March frosts, June's voracious beetles,
and the quenchless thirsts of August.

Ellen Bryant Voigt

Farm Wife

Dark as the spring river, the earth
opens each damp row as the farmer
swings the far side of the field.
The blackbirds flash their red
wing patches and wheel in his wake,
down to the black dirt; the windmill
grinds in its chain rig and tower.

In the kitchen, his wife is baking.
She stands in the door in her long white
gloves of flour. She cocks her head and
tries to remember, turns like the moon
toward the sea-black field. Her belly
is rising, her apron fills like a sail.
She is gliding now, the windmill churns
beneath her, she passes the farmer,
the fine map of the furrows.
The neighbors point to the bone-white
spot in the sky.
                    Let her float
like a fat gull that swoops and circles,

before her husband comes in for supper,
before her children grow up and leave her,
before the pulley cranks her down
the dark shaft, and the church blesses
her stone bed, and the earth seals
its black mouth like a scar.

MARGARET WALKER

Lineage

My grandmothers were strong.
They followed plows and bent to toil.
They moved through fields sowing seed.
They touched earth and grain grew.
They were full of sturdiness and singing.
My grandmothers were strong.

My grandmothers are full of memories
Smelling of soap and onions and wet clay
With veins rolling roughly over quick hands
They have many clean words to say.
My grandmothers were strong.
Why am I not as they?

DuBose Heyward

The Mountain Woman

Among the sullen peaks she stood at bay
And paid life's hard account from her small store.
Knowing the code of mountain wives, she bore
The burden of the days without a sigh;
And, sharp against the somber winter sky,
I saw her drive her steers afield each day.

Hers was the hand that sunk the furrows deep
Across the rocky, grudging southern slope.
At first youth left her face, and later, hope;
Yet through each mocking spring and barren fall,
She reared her lusty brood, and gave them all
That gladder wives and mothers love to keep.

And when the sheriff shot her eldest son
Beside his still, so well she knew her part,
She gave no healing tears to ease her heart;
But took the blow upstanding, with her eyes
As drear and bitter as the winter skies.
Seeing her then, I thought that she had won.

But yesterday her man returned too soon
And found her tending, with a reverent touch,
One scarlet bloom; and having drunk too much,
He snatched its flame and quenched it in the dirt.
Then, like a creature with a mortal hurt,
She fell, and wept away the afternoon.

FRED CHAPPELL

My Grandmother Washes Her Feet

I see her still, unsteadily riding the edge
Of the clawfoot tub, mumbling to her feet,
Musing bloodrust water about her ankles.
Cotton skirt pulled up, displaying bony
Bruised patchy calves that would make you weep.

Rinds of her soles had darkened, crust-colored—
Not yellow now—like the tough outer belly
Of an adder. In fourteen hours the most refreshment
She'd given herself was dabbling her feet in the water.

"You mightn't've liked John-Giles. Everybody knew
He was a mean one, galloping whiskey and bad women
All night. Tried to testify dead drunk
In church one time. That was a ruckus. Later
Came back a War Hero, and all the young men
Took to doing the things he did. And failed.
Finally one of his women's men shot him."

"What for?"

     "Stealing milk through fences. . . . That part
Of Family nobody wants to speak of.
They'd rather talk about fine men, brick houses,
Money. Maybe you ought to know, teach you

Something."

            "What *do* they talk about?"

                                    "Generals,
And the damn Civil War, and marriages.
Things you brag about in the front of Bibles.
You'd think there was arms and legs of Family
On every battlefield from Chickamauga
To Atlanta."

            "That's not the way it is?"

"Don't matter how it is. No proper way
To talk, is all. It was nothing they ever did.
And plenty they *won't* talk about . . . John-Giles!"

Her cracked toes thumped the tub wall, spreading
Shocklets. Amber toenails curled like shavings.
She twisted the worn knob to pour in coolness
I felt suffuse her body like a whiskey.

"Bubba Martin, he was another, and no
Kind of man. Jackleg preacher with the brains
Of a toad. Read the Bible upside down and crazy
Till it drove him crazy, making crazy marks
On doorsills, windows, sides of Luther's barn.
He killed hisself at last with a shotgun.
No gratitude for Luther putting him up
all those years. Shot so he'd fall down the well."

"I never heard."

"They never mention him.
Nor Aunt Annie, that everybody called
Paregoric Annie, that roamed the highways
Thumbing cars and begging change to keep
Even with her craving. She claimed she was saving up
To buy a glass eye. It finally shamed them
Enough, they went together and got her one.
That didn't stop her. She lugged it around
In a velvet-lined case, asking strangers
Please to drop it in the socket for her.
They had her put away. And that was that.
There's places Family ties just won't stretch to."

Born then in my mind a race of beings
Unknown and monstrous. I named them Shadow-Cousins,
A linked long dark line of them,
Peering from mirrors and gleaming in closets, agog
To manifest themselves inside myself.
Like discovering a father's cancer.
I wanted to search my body for telltale streaks.

"Sounds like a bunch of cow thieves."

           "Those too, I reckon,
But they're forgotten or covered over so well
Not even I can make them out. Gets foggy
When folks decide they're coming on respectable.
First thing you know, you'll have a Family Tree."

(I imagined a wind-stunted horse-apple.)

She raised her face. The moons of the naked bulb

flared in her spectacles, painting out her eyes.
In dirty water light bobbed like round soap.
A countenance matter-of-fact, age engraved,
Mulling in peaceful wonder petty annals
Of embarrassment. Gray but edged with brown
Like an old photograph, her hair shone yellow.
A tiredness mantled her fine energy.
She shifted, sluicing water under instep.

"O what's the use," she said. "Water seeks
Its level. If your daddy thinks that teaching school
In a white shirt makes him a likelier man,
What's to blame? Leastways, he won't smother
Of mule-farts or have to starve for a pinch of rainfall.
Nothing new gets started without the old's
Plowed under, or halfway under. We sprouted from dirt,
Though, and it's with you, and dirt you'll never forget."

"No Mam."

        "Don't you say me No Mam yet.
Wait till you get your chance to deny it."

Once she giggled, a sound like stroking muslin.

"You're bookish. I can see you easy a lawyer
Or a county clerk in a big white suit and tie,
Feeding the preacher and bribing the sheriff and the judge.
Second-generation-respectable
Don't come to any better destiny.
But it's dirt you rose from, dirt you'll bury in.
Just about the time you'll think your blood

Is clean, here will come dirt in a natural shape
you never dreamed. It'll rise up saying, Fred,
Where's that mule you're supposed to march behind?
Where's your overalls and roll-your-owns?
Where's your Blue Tick hounds and Domineckers?
Not all the money in this world can wash true-poor
True rich. Fatback just won't change to artichokes."

"What's artichokes?"

    "Pray Jesus you'll never know.
For if you do it'll be a sign you've grown
Away from what you are, can fly to flinders
Like a touch-me-not . . . I may have errored
When I said *true-poor*. It ain't the same
As dirt-poor. When you got true dirt you got
Everything you need . . . And don't you say me
Yes Mam again. You just wait."

       She leaned
And pulled the plug. The water circled gagging
To a bloody eye and poured in the hole like a rat.
I thought maybe their spirits had gathered there,
All my Shadow-Cousins clouding the water,
And now they ran to earth and would cloud the earth.
Effigies of soil, I could seek them out
By clasping soil, forcing warm rude fingers
Into ancestral jelly my father wouldn't plow.
I strained to follow them, and never did.
I never had the grit to stir those guts.
I never had the guts to stir that earth.

Emily Hiestand

Planting in Tuscaloosa

Three women are walking in Alabama.
My mother and I help my grandmother walk
around the field where she planted and raised.
As we circle the land I think of the way
women will sometimes stroke a belly with child.
My uncle's tractor combs the deep red clay.
      Now she wears a housecoat.

Summers, I stayed with her and rode the glider
on her porch—cement painted pink.
I watched her wave a paper fan printed
with pictures of Jesus in unbelievable colors.
She waved away the sulphur smells that blew
at night from the Warrior River paper mill.
Once a man reading Sunday papers
in my bed asked me if I had page twelve;
I said I didn't have it. Then he asked
for page fifty; I said I didn't have it.
Then he asked for page seventy-three
and I said, "Go fish," and we laughed
for ten minutes and made love and laughed.
Those laughs were courtesy of my grandmother.
She played Go Fish with me for hours,
managing a dumb wedge of cards
while I was mesmerized by the distinctions

between diamonds and hearts. How
could any adult love a child enough
to play a game like Go Fish for hours?
          Now she calls us to her room.

Every summer another tree was covered
by the swarming kudzu vines that grew
taller and taller than the men with machetes.
A glass kept on her Bible magnified the word.
The women snapped beans in Sister's parlor
and watched "As The World Turns" on TV.
"Laura, was Brian with you in church?"
Snap. Ping into the metal colanders.
I tried always to get the whole string off,
counting how many were right, two, then a goof.
How did she get the beans to snap so,
and always get the whole string off
and watch television and talk all the time.
          Now she is heaped with gladiolas.

Two women are walking in Alabama.
My mother and I walk arm and arm in her field.
The tractor harrows and dust begins to rise.
I stand ankle-deep in the field.
I am given her porcelain pitcher to keep.
Bits of clay cling to my feet.

Robert Gibbons

At Jo's Funeral

Though she is dead,
    and now we come to bury her,
    I wear no black.

I wear no black,
    instead green:
    to praise the gardens in her life,
    where spires of bulbs
    pushed early out of earth,
    done at last with the long wait.

I wear no black,
    instead gray:
    acknowledging ashes of fires
    that burned for her—
    kiln heat to season
    the clay of the vessel,
    sun warmth to mellow
    the liquor of God.

He Makes a House Call

Six, seven years ago
when you began to faint
I painted your leg with iodine

threaded the artery
with the needle and then the tube
pumped your heart with dye enough

to see the valve
almost closed with stone.
We were both under pressure.

Today, in your garden,
kneeling under the sticky fig tree
for tomatoes

I keep remembering your blood.
Seven, it was. I was just
beginning to learn the heart

inside out.
Afterward, your surgery
and the precise valve of steel

and plastic that still pops and clicks
inside like a ping-pong ball.
I should try

chewing tobacco sometime
if only to see how it tastes.
There is a trace of it at the corner

of your leathery smile
which insists that I see inside
the house: someone named Bill I'm supposed

to know; the royal plastic soldier
whose body fills with whiskey
and marches on a music box

How Dry I Am;
the illuminated 3-D Christ who turns
into Mary from different angles;

the watery basement,
the pills you take, the ivy
that may grow around the ceiling

if it must. Here, you
are in charge—of figs, beans,
tomatoes, life.

At the hospital, a thousand times
I have heard your heart valve open, close.
I know how clumsy it is.

But health is whatever works
and for as long. I keep thinking
of seven years without a faint

on my way to the car
loaded, loaded with vegetables,
I keep thinking of seven years ago

when you bled in my hands like a saint.

Before Tulips

The tulips have not bloomed
although the early balm of April
shoves up flares of jonquils
and splays the start of maple buds
to violet jacks.
I do not want the tulips to bloom
or my heart to break yet.
They do not merge,
the tulips stand apart
too red or yellow,
too varnished,
split bullets fused on green.
Their beauty and invective
stun me backward in a shock of praise.
Even the molting blue cannot caress them.

Alexis, my little friend,
magnificent woman's daughter,
you sleep through the wind at the open window,
the lawn beds singing the love of tulips,
their end of burial.

Your flower is still a rose,
and you sleep like the rose,
rose asleep in its red.

Bonnie Roberts

Take Me Down That Row
One More Time, Green-Eyed Boy

I always have plenty of green for you, cousin,
the green silk corn shucks of our childhood
piling us in Uncle's harvest wagon up to the moon
or your mama's peas and fried green tomatoes
tasting like hues of shade
beneath the fence-line tree
on the cotton picker's sack
when the noon bell rang.
And on days when work was done,
we sat on the fat pond moss of our playhouse rug
or ran through the tall meadow grass,
hiding, rolling, planning in the earth,
itching, powerful with chiggers, to be grown,
silly things,
and the summer blades cut our faces,
without pain.
In those days, sweet cuz,
even blood
ran green.

V.
FRUITS AND VEGETABLES

Coleman Barks

Summer Food

Green, the shape of a man,
with the insides of a woman,

they swim and dive around each other
in the boiling water, like porpoises.

O, to put the whole pod
of okra in the mouth.

Tomatoes, it is time to taste
ourselves, in these wet, red rooms,
the rooms of our mouths,
where lives the sigh
of language.

Corn, the tassels pull apart,
ears and silk, ears and silk and teeth,

Cantaloupe, a globe in tight webbing,
crisscross imprint. The onion underground,
in crumbs of dirt and old fabric.
Heat waves take form. Without panic or fear,
the air becomes visible.

Cucumbers, turning and sinking in the vinegar bowl.

I hold a head of cauliflower in my hand.

It's the head of someone whose name escapes,
which is not so strange. There are many names
for the ones we love, and wonderful to say:

Broccoli, Lettuce, Cabbage,
String Beans, Snow Peas, Pear,
Watermelon, Pomegranate, Plum.

Let us eat the solid forms of sunlight,
and walk around after supper
in the gold time,
loving each other and talking vegetables.

Becky Gould Gibson

Putting up Damson Preserves

You were right. I've never seen
such fruit, knobs the size of a man's thumb
clustered blue on every branch.
That old scrawny-necked tree shawled
in lichen lace I thought dead
you brought back, spread manure under
every spring till you died. Each year
it yields a few more pints. Your daughters
are grown, your sons have taken your place.

That's Marie at the sink seeding plums,
splitting each one along the crease.
You watched me watching the fruit,
taking it down to its sweetness.
You liked to lick foam from the spoon,
recalling the color of the dance dress
I wore in those cleaned out rooms.
But I'm not the girl you knew, nor
the woman either, here in the kitchen
with you gone off like steam.

Where your hands went I'm still smooth.
When you first came to me in the dark
I was scared, then you brought me close,
I thought I would fall, but where

you took me I could not fall enough—
split, unseeded, beyond blue to purple,
black, back to white, fruit to flower,
bee, beginning of the world.

Now I keep summer in jars, shelved
for pale winter tongues.
Sometimes I take one down, taste
the blue sweet all over again.

Robert Morgan

Full of the Moon

No one ever could explain why
the moon governed the crops, why things
fruiting above ground like beans
must be planted on the wax
and those bearing under soil
like carrots or potatoes should
be put out on the wane, and why
corn seeded on the full would go
tree high, all stalk and little ear,
and why peas started at the new
might not fill out their shells. It seemed
certain the force that plucked the tides
could interfere with vegetables
and cast its power and coldness
over enzyme and germ, that cells
could be stirred or starved by
answering ebbs and highs, and that
the pulse of it all, though not lunar,
was sensitive to the face of
earth's closest alien. But no one
ever said, while sun is life itself,
how the cool sister of night,
changing, ruled the summer kingdom,
though high and calm as strangest dream.

JAMES APPLEWHITE

Collards

Green hens perching the pole
   Of a row, concentric wings
Fly you down into soil.

You catch the rain like rings
   Where a pine stump tunnels
Time backward down roots' seasonings.

If roots rot to dark channels
   Mining the forest, your fiber
Threads grease in the entrails

Of families, whose bodies harbor
   Scars like rain on a hillslope,
Whose skin takes sheen like lumber

Left out in the weather. Old folk
   Seem sewed together by pulp
Of your green rope and smoke

From the cook fires boys gulp
   For dinner along roads in winter.
Collards and ham grease they drop

In the pot come back as we enter
　　The house whose porch shows a pumpkin.
This steam holds all we remember.

Sweet potatoes clot in a bin,
　　Common flesh beneath this skin
Like collards. Grainy-sweet, kin.

Marcia Camp

Farmer's Market

It isn't okra cut small and tender the way
      we know it should be, or
tomatoes whose imperfections declare them
      simon-pure, or
peas bursting from their purple hulls
(their remembered anthem sung on summer-
      morning streets,
"Peas . . ." with soft refrain, "already shelled")—
we come for none of these, though we ask the
      price at each tailgate.
We're here to see hardy faces (our parents and
      grandparents with different features)
smile a warranty on produce knowing hands and
      bent backs coaxed to life.
We tender crisp dollar bills, drop quarters
      into calloused palms and
purchase affirmation.
For we need to hear the vernacular of hill,
      prairie and delta in
words carefully weeded from our city talk,

have our nostrils sting from manure on boots,
smell musk of frying bacon lingering in work shirts.
Only here can we feel Dallis grass switch our ankles,
        blackberry briers claw our legs,
hear the night call of the whippoorwill,
        see its red eye pierce the dark, and
know that we did not dream childhood.

Anne George

Picking Tomatoes on Sand Mountain

The pickup bounces
up a corrugated road
through patchwork, red,
gold, strips of lavender. We
touch our mouths carefully
to styrofoam cups of coffee,
sing "On the Road Again."
Then the sign "Pick Your Own"
and a million tomatoes
reflecting the sun.

We are early, the only ones.
We take our baskets, move
down the rows. Ripe tomatoes
drop with the slightest of twists.
Spaghetti sauce, I think, ketchup.

At the lip of the bluff we rest,
watch clouds bank in the west.
You bite a tomato, juice
runs down your chin. I
lie back against the warm rocks,
watch hawks wheeling.

Listen, for whatever, I forgive you.

James Applewhite

Storm in the Briar Patch

In obedience and ignorance, okra
　　stalks, gaunt as prisoners, stand
where screens only keep the flies in.
　　Dry season and the boy's father
slaps him for no reason it seems—
　　rutted landscape fallen to ruin,
pokeweed veined like a hand
　　where the scraps of laundry hang,
flap like the wrung-necked rag of
　　a chicken in its arcs. Storm
seems a long time coming and strong
　　when it dooms down. Spark
crack connects the sky and land
　　with copper-green scar in the eye,
as the cat trembles, the three fish
　　wait to be cleaned. The lean-tos
lean into the wind, lean as bean-
　　poles, the beans dangling, jangled
like wind chimes, while farmers damn
　　the hail as it holes tobacco: broad
as banana leaves, like small roofs but
　　pierced now, a punctured infantry.
After, he goes the rounds of his fields, each
　　hill shredded, a mimic-man, a sham of

what life might be—ghost of a crop to go
     up from a match in cloud and
gesture, not shiver here, broken, long
     hours of raising ruined in his eyes.

Charles Edward Eaton

Squashes

Like beheaded geese plucked to their yellow skin they lie in the
    shade
Of an obscene but stalwart little forest of thick leaves,
Lost in all that heat, in a world they never made.

Brought into the house they lose their murdered, meat-shop look—
I place them along the stone wall on the porch,
Their necks entwined like abstracts of little yellow mandolins
        accompanied by a book.

In a manner of speaking I have arranged for their rescue—
They are handsome as a Braque, accented by that important,
Lyric-looking volume with the jacket of dark blue.

Always and always the suspicion mounts
As we accumulate our world around us and see it rot
That, given the given, it is what we do with a thing that counts.

Which is not to say that now or ever one will quite be done
With whatever dreams itself to be in us at first glance,
Little glutted, yellow-bellied, murdered geese lying in the sun.

But if on closer look the mandolins are warted, not quite so sleekly
    gold,
And the wind shallows through the pages of the book,
We shall have made our passions for a little while do as they are told.

MARGARET GIBSON

The Onion

Mornings when sky is white as dried gristle
and the air's unhealthy, coast
smothered, and you gone
                I could stay in bed
and be the woman who aches for no reason, each day
a small death of love, cold rage for dinner,
coffee and continental indifference
at dawn.
          Or dream lazily a market day—
bins of fruit and celery, poultry strung up,
loops of garlic and peppers. I'd select one
yellow onion, fist-sized, test its sleek
hardness, haggle and settle a fair price.

Yesterday, a long day measured by shovel
and mattock, a wrestle with roots—
calm and dizzy when I bent over to loosen my shoes
at the finish—I thought
                if there were splendors,
what few there were, knowledge of them
in me like fire in flint,
I would have them . . .
             and now I'd say the onion,
I'd have that, too. The work it took,
the soup it flavors, the griefs
innocently it summons.

Robert Penn Warren

Riddle in the Garden

My mind is intact, but the shapes
of the world change, the peach
has released the bough and at last
makes full confession, its *pudeur*
has departed like peach-fuzz wiped off, and

We now know how the hot sweet-
ness of flesh and the juice-dark hug
the rough peach-pit, we know its most
suicidal yearnings, it wants
to suffer extremely, it

Loves God, and I warn you, do not
touch that plum, it will burn you, a blister
will be on your finger, and you will
put the finger to your lips for relief—oh, do
be careful not to break that soft

Gray bulge of fruit-skin of blister, for
exposing that inwardness will
increase your pain, for you
are part of the world. You think
I am speaking in riddles. But I am not, for

The world means only itself.

NAOMI SHIHAB NYE

Going for Peaches, Fredericksburg, Texas

Those with experience look for a special kind.
Red globe, the skin slips off like a fine silk camisole.
Boy breaks one open with his hands. Yes, it's good,
my old relatives say, but we'll look around.
They want me to stop at every peach stand
between Stonewall and Fredericksburg,
leave the air conditioner running,
jump out and ask the price.

Coming up here they talked about
the best ways to die. One favors a plane crash,
but not over a city. One wants to make sure
her grass is watered when she goes.
Ladies, ladies! This peach is fine,
it blushes on both sides.
But they want to keep driving.

In Fredericksburg the houses are stone,
they remind me of wristwatches, glass polished,
years ticking by in each wall.
I don't like stone, says one. What if it fell?
I don't like Fredericksburg, says the other.
Too many Germans driving too slow.

She herself is German as Stuttgart.
The day presses forward, wearing complaints
like charms on its bony wrist.

Actually ladies (I can't resist),
I don't think you wanted peaches after all,
you just wanted a nip of scenery,
some hills to tuck behind your heads.
The buying starts immediately, from a scarfed woman who says
I gave up teachin' for peachin'.
She has us sign the guest book.
One aunt insists on re-loading into her own box,
so she can see the fruit on the bottom.
One rejects any slight bruise.
But Ma'am, the seller insists, nature isn't perfect.
Her hands are spotted, like a peach.

On the road, cars weave loose patterns between lanes.
We will float in flowery peach-smell
back to our separate kettles, our private tables and knives,
and line up the bounty,
deciding which ones go where.
A canned peach, says one aunt, lasts ten years.
She was 87 last week. But a frozen peach
tastes better on ice cream.
Everything we have learned so far,
the stages of ripening alive in our skins,
on a day that was real to us, that was summer,
motion going out and memory coming in.

CATHARINE SAVAGE BROSMAN

Peaches

I

Cobblers, pies, preserves, salads, peaches
and cream—even a pulpy ice:
since a spring without a freeze
turned early blossoms into this surfeit
of fruit, we have eaten peaches
every way we know, not forgetting
right from the branch, fuzz barely washed
under the faucet. Take one, now
from the bowl, a world ripe
with the continents of summer's color.

II

Long, unwrinkled days lead to evenings
nearly as long, and cooler, when phoebes
describe arcs around the trellises,
and rising flycatchers belie the stillness
of the air. Today we picked some more,
filling old-fashioned jars
with juice and golden flesh—gathering too
a little weariness, but sweet,
as after playing with a child
or singing late to friendship's music.

III

After the immoderate midday sun,
my father was shade, measure,
and perspective. If one pail of peaches
was brought in on a summer's afternoon,
it was enough for him, knotting
the different threads of need and pleasure.
This fruit preserved is husbanding happiness
for future weeks; something of autumn
is already in their ripening,
the reconciliation of reason and love.

IV

The clean and candid light of Spanish rooms,
a simple love affair in summer clothes—
both quick and beautiful,
these call for ceremonial, like fruit
served on a blue-willow plate. Is this not
funereal, finally—the unnamed seed
of dying in even the freshest peach,
and all our rituals the savoring
of ourselves, most perishable,
but delighting in what resembles us?

JACK BUTLER

Preserves

Great love goes mad to be spoken: you went out
to the ranked tent-poles of the butterbean patch,
picked beans in the sun. You bent, and dug
the black ground for fat purple turnips.
You suffered the cornstalk's blades, to emerge
triumphant with grain. You spent all day in a coat
of dust, to pluck the difficult word
of a berry, plunk in a can. You brought home
voluminous tribute, cucumbers, peaches,
five-gallon buckets packed tightly with peas,
cords of sugar-cane, and were not content.

You had not yet done the pure, the completed,
the absolute deed. Out of that vegetable ore,
you wrought miracles: snap-beans broke
into speech, peas spilled from the long slit pod
like pearls, and the magical snap of your nail
filled bowls with the fat white coinage of beans.

Still, you were unfinished. Now fog swelled
in the kitchen, your hair wilted like vines.
These days drove you half-wild—you cried, sometimes,
for invisible reasons. In the yard, out of your way,
we played in the leaves and heard
the pressure-cooker blow out its musical shriek.

Then it was done: you had us stack up the jars
like ingots, or books. In the dark of the shelves,
quarts of squash gave off a glow like late sun.

That was the last we thought of your summer
till the day that even the johnson grass died.
Then, bent over sweet relish and black-eyed peas,
over huckleberry pie, seeing the dog outside
shiver with cold, we would shiver, and eat.

R. H. W. Dillard

Meditation for a Pickle Suite

Morning: the soft release
As you open a jar of pickles.
The sun through the window warm
And moving like light through brine,
The shadows of pickles swim the floor.
And in the tree, flowing down the chimney,
The songs of fresh birds clean as pickles.
Memories float through the day
Like pickles, perhaps sweet gherkins.
The past rises and falls
Like curious pickles in dark jars,
Your hands are sure as pickles,
Opening dreams like albums,
Pale Polish pickles.
Your eyes grow sharp as pickles,
Thoughts as green, as shining
As rows of pickles, damp and fresh,
Placed out in the afternoon sun.

GEORGE SCARBROUGH

Root Cellar

Opening inward
the door makes an angle
with the wall.
It's the angle
that interests me.
More than the tooth-
marked potato
always lying just inside
on the dirt floor.

I have only
to close the door
to banish the angle
and disencumber myself
of the salient problem,
pocked potato included.
It's a short way out
to the tunnel's end
where night snow falls
and things die in the cold.

I know enough to know
a straight angle shuts in
more than it shuts out
when it appertains

to root cellar doors,
and a right angle runs
quickest to distance.

But the peaches stand
on sagging shelves
at the very back
of the earthen hole.
In webbed and powdered
Mason glass
they shine in rows
like faint heat lightning
filtered through clouds
from below the rim
of a hot, black world.

But it isn't summer.
Not by a month and a half.
Not by a frost and a freeze.
I've told you that already.

So I go tiptoeing in.

God, don't let
the wind move the door,
if it is the wind!
Let it be steady.
Neither increase
nor decrease
the degree of my trouble!

O I act like a thief
with my own wealth
in the prowling dark
and, apprehended, flee,
hooking the door
shut behind me
with a flying foot.

I never reach for the knob.
it might shake hands.
Never disturb the potato.
It might, God grant, be
the same one next time!

The jars come clean
in the beautiful snow.
And, one in each hand,
I traverse the dark white yard
into the houseglow,
carrying sliced yellow quarts
of harvest moon.

Volunteer

Praise what survives
its season of domestication
and sprouts along the margin,
among next year's crop.

Aggressive species ignore
fences and the boundary lines
of rotation to emigrate.

Praise blooded varieties returning
to the wild.

Spontaneous replanting be praised. Let
self-sowers reverdure the earth.

Let every garden and tiergarten and
sunken eden leak
breeds that multiply
to the limits of resource.

Praise all escapes
and trailing shrubs, runners that
spill out of culture
and reseed themselves.

Let volunteers find accommodation.

VI.
YARDS AND GARDENS

Jonathan Williams

The Flower-Hunter in the Fields

(for Agnes Arber)

a flame azalea, mayapple, maple, thornapple
plantation

a white cloud in the eye
of a white horse

a field of bluets moving
below the black suit
of William Bartram

bluets; or "Quaker Ladies," or some say
"Innocence"

bluets and the blue of gentians and
Philadelphia blue laws . . .

high hills,

stone cold
sober

as October

ANDREW GLAZE

Buick

I am sitting
on the creek edge with my
feet in the water.
There is an oak log crossing the creek.
Off to the left, a path where animals run.
Possums and coons are running along it
through a forest where the creek
is running like a snake
through the middle of the trees.
The creek and the path and the forest
are running through me.

Among wild delphinium making thin blue-bell towers,
"Spring," says Sweet William.
He shines like pink, cheap jewelry
flung in the coarse grass everywhere.
Dogwood blazes in sheets of white crosses.
My father is digging at something
with his wild orchid pick.
An old Buick sits in the clearing
splendid with green plush seats,
and there is a garden at the edge of the forest.
Now, as I was in the forest,
I am becoming the garden.
Pick up the wet sack with the wild orchids.
Reach them high up into the back of the Buick.

Jane Gentry

A Garden in Kentucky

Under the fluorescent sun
inside the Kroger, it is always
southern California. Hard avocados
rot as they ripen from the center out.
Tomatoes granulate inside their hides.
But by the parking lot, a six-tree orchard
frames a cottage where winter has set in.

Pork fat seasons these rooms.
The wood range spits and hisses,
limbers the oilcloth on the table
where an old man and an old woman
draw the quarter moons of their nails,
shadowed still with dirt,
across the legends of seed catalogues.

Each morning he milks the only goat
inside the limits of Versailles. She feeds
a rooster that wakes up all the neighbors.
Through dark afternoons and into night
they study the roses' velvet mouths
and the apples' bright skins
that crack at the first bite.

When thaw comes, the man turns up
the sod and, on its underside, ciphers

roots and worms. The sun like an angel
beats its wings above their grubbing.
Evenings on the viny porch they rock,
discussing clouds, the chance of rain.
Husks in the dark dirt fatten and burst.

Carol Prejean Zippert

Going Home

I'm going home. I've decided
To catch a glimpse
of a small woodframe house
lined with roses, azaleas, camellias
and peppermint tea
I'm going home
to a backyard forever with the sounds
of baby chicks, ducks and
an occasional pig
A backyard housing rabbits
a vegetable garden
a chinaberry tree
and perpetually covered laundry lines
I'm going home, I've decided
To climb to the top of the spreading oak
and spy on the neighbors
or maybe just to sit under the fig trees
I'm going home
To be consumed by the nightly aroma
of freshly cooked breads
from the around-the-corner bakery
that also produced the cinnamon rolls for
after-Sunday-morning-Mass breakfast
I'm going home, I've decided
To the kite-flying winds of March

which threatened to topple us off
the tallest tombs in the graveyard across the street
To April even when it didn't bring Easter
To summer flavors of newly cut grass in June
To the brown hightop shoes, coveralls and
a birthday in March, April, May, June,
August, September, October and November
I'm going home
to holiday December
To my Mother's gumbo after midnight Mass
and wonder again why the day after Christmas
wasn't as much fun as Christmas Day
I'm going home
to when it's not yet payday time
and supper is cornbread and syrup
I'm going home, I've decided
To the constant sound of my Mother's voice
her quilting voice
her cooking and cleaning voice
her chicken-feeding voice
her working-for-the-church voice
her voice to my father which invariably brought
the clicking sound
of a door closing behind him
I'm going home
to six siblings crowded in two beds
laughing, playing, fussing, crying,
growing and saying goodbye
I'm going home
to the piano in the dining room
proudly displaying generations of photographs
To the attic fan I feared would suck me up

To the graveyard across the street
that tolerated our nighttime games
I'm going home, I've decided
To smell the 4 p.m. coffee
awaiting my father's return from work
I'm going home
to follow behind him
not too closely as he checked
the vegetable garden, the roses, the azaleas,
the camellias and the peppermint tea
I'm going home, I've decided
I'm going home
but I've not decided
when

EMILY HIESTAND

Making Our Garden

There are givens—pliable days
when trees and rain flow in the fields
like paint from tubes. As for us, we try too.
We built a terrace: two inches of gravel,
two inches of sand, used a leveling screed,
pavers on top in the basketweave pattern—
still, not like pictures in the Time-Life book
where edges are straight, and the gravel even.

Pictures can be so perfect.
We sawed railroad ties to the right lengths
for a bed of roses. I told him about roses:
hybrids with names, the many names of good.
You can order from a book or heft
a balled specimen from the nursery lot,
any one you want for your garden:
Alchymist, Pax, Gypsy, Joy,
Mrs. Merriweather Post, Hope.

Nothing named Doubt or Dismay or Mean
grows tinier and tinier, more and more perfect
near the center. We set out pachysandra.
It's hard to set out pachysandra.
The plant has shallow runners so you use
up too much space on the first one,

then you must twist the next one around;
by the third you're leaving root exposed
or digging up the other two.

It would have to be planned like
a Celtic knot: each runner arranged
in a geometric plot (trial and error
or use a ruler); then chalk in the plan,
revise if necessary; next dig
out the lines, some deeper than others
for overlaying; put in the plants, cover.
That's not the way we do it at all.
Yet, in time the roots entwine ingenious
under a sweet ceiling of dwarf umbrellas
about three inches off the ground.

RODNEY JONES

Dirt

I am not a saint. All
that I am coming to
is crusting under my nails.
I am dragging my dull hoe
through the peppercorns
and letting the malathion snow
from the twin clouds
of my rubber gloves.
Here I am, the marshal
come to rescue the schoolgirls!
Here I am, the fat messiah
of the family! My aphids
twitch, of abstraction
and consequence bereft. They
linger in the narcotic hair
of the okra like glue,
their love's labor multiplied.
But I am merely exhausted
and hot. Sweat
clings to my brow
like thorns, my face
is flawed with the maps
of continents I shall never see.
My cleanliness is next to sleep.
When I look into the mirror,

when I lower my head
into the cool basin,
it is mercy I think of.
I keep trying
to grab some purity
in the water pouring over my hands.

DANNYE ROMINE POWELL

Primer on Digging

Memory is the characteristic art form
of those who have just decided to die
and those who have just decided to live.
—Daniel Stern, *The Suicide Academy*

Listen: when you dig
in the garden
expect to be bitten.
Those fish heads you buried
last spring endure beyond seasons,
breeding their own subtleties.
Your fingers will encounter
the slow growth of moss,
the spasms of slugs
recoiling from salt.
Go further: one mild earthworm
is not sufficient to measure the world.
Hard by the brick wall
the roly-poly unfurls,
a bolus of damp memory
assaulting your nostrils.
Wait. Don't reach for the spade.
You must touch the white root
with your fingers, follow
its search for cool water.

Now that your hands are submerged
notice how the dark treasures
quicken like dreams
beneath your swollen fingertips.

ANDREW HUDGINS

Compost: An Ode

Who can bring a clean thing
out of an unclean?
—Job 14: 4

The beauty of the compost heap is not
the eye's delight.
    Eyes see too much.
       They see
blood-colored worms
     and bugs so white they seem
to feed off ghosts. Eyes
    do not see the heat
that simmers in
    the moist heart of decay—
in its unmaking,
    making fire,
       just hot
enough to burn
    itself. In summer, the heap
burns like a stove. It can—almost—hurt you.
I've held my hand inside the fire and counted
one, two, three,
    four.
     I cannot hold it there.

Give it to me, the heat insists. *It's mine.*
I yank it back and wipe it on my jeans
as if

      I'd really heard the words.

               And eyes

cannot appreciate

         sweet vegetable rot,
how good it smells

         as everything dissolves,
dispersing

      back from thing

            into idea.

From our own table we are feeding it
what we don't eat. Orange rind and apple core,
corn husks,

      and odds and ends the children smear
across their plates—we feed them all into the slow,
damp furnace of decay. Leaves curl at edges,
buckle,

      collapsing down into their centers,
as everything turns loose its living shape
and blackens, gives up

         what it once was
to become dirt. The table scraps
and leafage join,

        indistinguishable,
the way that death insists it's all the same,
while life

      must do a million things at once.
The compost heap is both—life, death—a slow
simmer,

             a leisurely collapsing of
the thing
             into its possibilities—
both bean and hollyhock, potato, zinnia, squash:
the opulence
             of everything that rots.

Henry Taylor

Buildings and Grounds

(for Richard Dillard)

The house we moved into has been landscaped
   so that it has the portable, plastic look
   of a Sears, Roebuck toy farm.

All up and down our street, the same minor artist seems
   to have been at work; our neighbors' lawns are
   watered and mowed truly until they are carpets,

their shrubs are lovingly trimmed and shaped
   into green velvet eggs and spheres.
   Our neighbors watch us like hawks,

wondering whether we have the equipment,
   the know-how, the spirit, to strive with them
   as they strive with their landscapes.

Oh, let me bring my home from the South to this street!
   I will let the grass grow until it is knee-high,

I will import chickens and a blue-tick hound to trample
   the grass and dig bone-holes and scratch-holes,

I will set up on cinderblocks in the front yard

a '38 Ford with no tires or headlights,
    to shelter the hound and the chickens,

I will sit in the gutted driver's seat
    with a bottle of Old Mr. Mac, glaring at my
    neighbors, reading aloud from *God's Little Acre*,

I will be a prophet of wildness and sloth!

But the Puritan gaze of my neighbors cuts through
    my desperate vision of home—my dream house
    will not flourish here.

I will spend my rapidly declining years
    reading the labels on bags of crabgrass killer,

pushing my lawn mower until my front yard
    is as smooth as a green on a golf course,

clipping and shaping my landlord's opulent shrubs.

But don't misunderstand me—I have not been
    converted; I will still make something
    to sustain me here in this alien land.

I will plant mint in the flowerbeds beside
    the Shasta daisies we brought from Monticello,

I will set up a croquet course on the front lawn
    with a slender drink-stand at each wicket
    to hold my frosty mint juleps,

I will station an iron jockey by the driveway
    to stare back into the pitiless eyes
    of my neighbors' pink plastic flamingoes,

I will keep a Tennessee Walking horse in the garage
    and give him a foxhound for company,

I will stand out front in a white linen suit
    surveying my plantation,

I will plant a magnolia tree.

But now, at the height of my visionary ecstasy,
    the telephone rings. It is the man
    next door, calling to let me know

that my sprinkler is turned up too high
    and is sprinkling the seats of his convertible.

I go out to turn down the water, and I see
    that the cedar needs trimming again,
    that the elm twigs need to be raked.

I will do those things. I will hoe and trench
    and weed, I will mow the grass.
    I have moved in here now,

and I have to do what I can.

Miller Williams

Politics

Mowing the lawn, having done with a tangle
of briar, with yellow jackets in the eaves,
he is imposing order, but he leaves
some ragged grass where fences make an angle,
trapping a small shadow most of the day.
There, in the swarming morning, circling twice,
his dog turns herself intently clockwise
then drops on the flattened grass. In this way
she reshapes the world to suit a hound.
A square yard of his yard he leaves to her
because he sees that both of them are bound
as Jesus, Jefferson, and Caesar were
(as all people are, and some small friends)
to change a stubborn world to fit their ends.

Helen F. Blackshear

Lazy Gardener

Weeds have invaded my garden.
Queen Anne's lace embroiders the edges.
Lavender primroses trespass in
cracks of the pavement.
Adjuratum chokes the chrysanthemums
and the grass surrendered to
dandelions long ago.

Everywhere, everywhere honeysuckle
hems the hedges, breathing out
sweetness so strong
it drowns my senses.

I used to fight the weeds
with torn nails and scraped hands.
A few skirmishes I won,
but they always came back
stronger than ever.

Now grudgingly I give
them growing space.
Defeated in battle,
I sit in my garden chair
and take some pleasure in
the glowing color
that delights the eye.
Weeds and I at last have come to terms.

George Garrett

The Mower

A week of rain has let my lawn run wild:
a prophet's beard, a mob with swarming blades,
except where, here and there, like a bad child,
a lone tongue flutters pure derision.

Well then, it's time for cutting, it appears.
Time to meet force with force, to roll
a keen and leveling weight on ragged sneers,
to snip off foolish tongues and shut them up.

And so I sweat behind my lawnmower knowing
prophet's head will haunt me and these slaves
will own my acres and, despite all mowing,
green tongues will bronx the air above my grave.

James Mersmann

Letting the Garden Go

Sluggish and fat in sweating midsummer,
I can only half remember how much hope
I sowed lush with the seeds
in early spring—the imagined vines
and fruit swollen heavy above the hoed loam.
And how the garden did for a time spring up
gay in its new leaf promise and blossom
with me at its center. Its loveliness,
its green symmetries and hubbub of bees
I loved more than any hoped-for harvest.
But could anyone, breaking the first brief rhubarb
from its hub before the heat burned the leaves back,
not have dreamed largesse of pies, rows
of preserves awaiting sweetened winter?
I did think, yes, there would be more
than just a few unbitten berries
stolen from under the gun
of the blue jay's bitching.
Now with a flat blade, August bats
all green back down, except the weeds that leap
up like scholars seeking national reputations,
strangling the light, breeding pustules
and smutboils on the sweetcorn. Wilt and blight
blast cucurbit and bean, cankerworm and mold
promote themselves among the melons.

Gnawed tomatoes, chipmunk bitten,
bleed like Goya's wounded. The garden's heart
pivots in a mandala of pestilence.
It would be easy to turn and walk away,
choosing exile at the garden's edge. I could
write it off, leave it to the slugs,
let the kudzu extend her limitless insinuations,
inexorably greedy, all-swallowing and quick.
I don't want to ponder all the hacking
and flailing, all the poisons
and sacks of shit it will take
to bring the garden back.
No doubt every man's August was always like this.
Has anyone made it to autumn unstung by the blow fly
that flowers from the dead? Among the bitten leaves
I understand the ancient ultimatum—only by sweat
and bitter love will you make things grow.
Today I must take hold or let the garden go.

Dave Smith

In the Yard, Late Summer

In the yard the plum tree, wild
with a late summer wind,
shakes its thousand planets
of sweet flesh.
Does it mean to resist
this gush that drops
one order of things
into another? It keels,
leaning at forces we can't
see, can't know the edge of.
Its memory keeps only two
commands: this lives, this
dies from the licking sun.
There is no metaphor
to reveal what it has known
in its brooding years.
We watch the purple fruit fall
as leaves shear and snap
and nail themselves to light.
Between us the wind
is a word seeking a shape,
hovering in passion
and risen from the ground
of memory clenched
in roots and long tendrils.

Hearing that, knowing ourselves
wingless and bestial, we wait
for the sun to blow out,
for the return of that first
morning of pink blossoms
when we saw the dark stains
of our feet printing
what we were on that
dew-bed of the world.
The tree, too, waits
in its old unraveling
toward a naked silence,
its language wild and shocked.

CHARLES EDWARD EATON

Crepe Myrtle

This is the myrtle of the South,
Creped and colored like the watermelon's inner flesh.
It burns the oil of branches, and, in the dry wind-thresh,
Ignites the air of August, month of wasted summer and of drouth.

The sweating florid faces look ready to explode:
They, too, from the same earth. They, too, from the same earth.
In the blazing prism of afternoon, death and birth
Touch but never fuse with the eternity of the road.

The myrtle and hot faces in the brazen air,
By suction from the green, from the wax-melting flesh, with love
       or lust,
Bloom, surge, and throb what will not be the dust
Until the white and phantom road is not and never will be there.

JOHN GOULD FLETCHER

Late Summer

Against the sky, a cloud-white bowl of flame,
The trees stand out, in masses of dark green;
Dizzy sunlight, fainting shadow,
To the distance dimly seen.

Great billows of haze rise up, slowly uncoil
Their heavy folds in silence. Underneath the leaves
The heat consumes the dew. A swallow darting
Skims, brushing the brown eaves.

Weedy gardens rank, neglected, smoulder
With ragweed, thistle, purple and scarlet flowers:—
Like gypsy girls they are staring
Through eyes unquiet and sombre,
Down the long hollow silences of the hours:—

Seeking for something long ago vanished and forgotten,
Something that time has now taken away, and fate no more will
     bring;
The hour before the blossom of life fell and the apple of earth went
     rotten,
The passionate, shrill, riotous hour of the waking of the spring.

A Sort of Adagio

In the evening
in the summer
in most mid-size cities
people walk after supper,
a light supper of chicken and fruit.
Pasta and wine.

In most yards
they will see at least one bed of flowers
or variegated plants
a sprinkler ticking slowly
over freshly cut grass

children tiptoeing over the lawn,
jar in hand,
intent upon faint, blooming
lightning bugs.

Joggers pass
with a steady *humpback, humpback.*
A dog or cat headed home or away,
depending on evening prospects,
eyes a walker suspiciously
and then moves on.

Only now and then
something unusual
something almost fantastic—
a woman walking a ferret on a leash
across a football field.
And for a moment, a brief moment,
the walker believes the world was created
precisely for these walks,

for these eyes, these ears,
this nose taking everything in.
The mind gone simple.
The body gone to seed.

The Garden

The garden is a book about the gardener.

Her thoughts, set down in vivid greenery,
The green light and the gold light nourish.
Firm sentences of grapevine, boxwood paragraphs,
End-stops of peonies and chrysanthemums,
Cut drowsy shadows on the paper afternoon.

Out of their hiding places the humid twilight
Lures the stars. The perfumes of the grass
Draw like cool curtains across the mind
And what the mind is certain it is certain of.

So that the twilight fragrances are clearly audible,
The garden stroking the senses with slow roses.
Bats ramble overhead, tacking from star
To early star as if putting in at ports of call.
And then the Chinese lantern is lit as it was in childhood,
As central in that place as an island lighthouse.

The gardener is a book about her garden.
She walks among these leaves as easy as morning
Come to scatter its robins and tender noises.
As the plants inhale the morning and its green light,
The book is open once again that was never shut.
What now we do not know we shall never know.

PATRICIA HOOPER

After Gardening

The last seeds have been planted,
and shadow has fallen, over
the long rows. In the loose shingle
the wrens in their tiny nest sing
when the mother comes with their food.

Tired from planting, I'm lying
in the soft grass, listening.
I recognize the dove, the purple finch,
and the cardinal's *What cheer, cheer, cheer* . . . .

I want to rest here and savor
the first evening of summer,
its delicate green musk. All winter
I looked out my window as if at a blank page,
planning the story of flowers.

Now the ruffled blue iris
joins the poppy with its frivolous orange heart
and the black scar at the center.
I can hardly remember
how I woke in the nights and wept

over something unchangeable.
This year, for the first time,
I noticed the early crocus without elation.

But now the habitual tasks
have carried me out here: weeds
and the work of planting have left me
in the last natural light,

a light I can still see by.
Overhead, in the thin branches,
strands of the day are wound
with the pink threads of the evening,

and nearby, on the fence post,
a thrush is singing, busy with its life.

A Charleston Garden

I love old gardens best—
tired old gardens
that rest in the sun.

There the rusty tamarisk
and knotted fig trees
lean on the wall,
and paper whites break rank
to wander carelessly
among tall grasses.
The yellow roses
slip from the trellis,
and the wistaria goes adventuring
to the neighboring trees.

The forgotten comfort
of the wilderness comes again.
The legend of the twisted walks
is broken,
and the marble seats are green
like woodland banks.

Gerald Barrax

Gift

What does it mean
that there is a snake lying among the wild strawberries;
   Spring has laid smooth stones
     at the edge of the pool;
   there are birds who see farther at night
     than the warm things under cover of purple leaves?
Some god has bitten this mottled apple.
We swim in these summer days, its juices.
What does it matter where the snake hides:
   I was out of place until a blue jay
   in return for my seed
   left that black banded feather from his wing
   in my back yard.

Jennifer Horne

Preservation of Life

(for Michael Bridges)

Michael, age six, stares unbelieving
at the green tomato hornworm,

the size of his little finger,
alive but unmoving,

covered with a white quilt:
parasitized by wasp larvae.

 This boy who draws aliens
with long purple arms,

skeletal stick men,
robot monster killers

stands in the high grass, transfixed
by this nightmare come to life.

"It's alive," he whispers.
"Nature's way," we say.

His mother and I go back to weeding.
Talking food, our mouths water:

salmon steaks with dill sauce,
fresh snap beans,

slices of golden tomatoes
topped with purple basil.

Michael squats in a corner of the garden,
his back a shield.

Carefully he picks the larvae off,
one by one, squashing them

with the rubber toe of his sneaker.
He looks back to be sure

he's unobserved in his labor.
We absorb ourselves in dodging fire ants.

Lazy with years,
what can we do but honor his impulse,

shut, for once, our platitudinous mouths?
Michael is saving life as he sees it,

and this saves more of him
than any common understanding will allow.

Basil

There in Fiesole it was always fresh
In the laneway where the spry grandfather
Tipped you his smile in the earliest wash
Of sunlight, piling strawberries high and higher
In a fragile pyramid of edible air.
Light down the years, the same sun rinses your dark
Hair over and over with brightness where
You kneel to stir the earth among thyme and chard,
Rosemary and the gathering of mints,
The rough leaf picked for tea this summer noon,
The smooth one saved for *pesto* in the winter,
For the cold will come, though you turn to me soon,
Your eyes going serious green from hazel,
Your quick hand on my face the scent of basil.

PETER HUGGINS

The Sadness of Gardens

Nothing sadder anywhere than this:
A garden at the end of summer.

Gone are the tomatoes and beans,
The broccoli and lettuce, the squash,

Melons and peppers, all that rich promise
Earlier in the year. But even as

The rose petals fall and the hydrangeas
Brown and wither, they are preparing

For next year's crop, for return from rest,
For warm weather, turned earth, spring.

CATHARINE SAVAGE BROSMAN

Cleaning the Shed

Something should be done to show out
the old year; inside, work aplenty
waits, or one could celebrate with
an early cheer the sense of change;
but I must look in at what remains
of the year's promises to myself.
Newspapers overflow that old crock,
better fit for moonshine; half-filled
with dirt, pots and jars line a rack;
webby marks on the single pane trace
last summer's spiders. For weeks,
I have walked in a net of broken toys,
fallen rakes and brooms, and watched
the sun's motions grow short; now
in the declining afternoon, little time
is left. This is no domestic rage,
no charade to please the neighbors,
but a gesture to myself, reminding me
of the liens on us, less possessing
than possessed, unless we learn how
to jettison what is outworn. Around
the door, the wind stirs, scattering
twigs from the cedar; birds sort through
the rest of fall. I will pour out
the soil for new worms, cart the trash

for burning, discard the impediments
to plain steps, and clear a few shelves
in my mind—needing to deny Mammon
in at least one way before its trap
consumes me, and make a spot for new
growth, waking in the earth's bones.

Loretta Cobb

Transplanted

(for Fred Bonnie)

Years ago, my window overlooked
a formal garden turned to thicket.
Daffodils and lilies
some woman's hands had patted
into this world
pushed through briars and vines
year after year—untended.
Peeping from the tangled mystery,
they announced her legacy.

Today, I watch a young man
thrash the flower beds.
The snarling instrument
shears the sage green shoots
before the blooms appear.

I ask if I can dig them up
and smooth the earth
where I recover
patient embryonic tubers.
They heave a brief contented sigh

and rest again beside my mother's grave.
I dig deep and tap them gently as she patted me,
knowing they'll rip their way
out of spring earth—blood red clay—
to stand erect with purple throats and
creamy petals softer than an infant's skin.

PATTIANN ROGERS

Finding the Tattooed Lady
in the Garden

Circus runaway, tattooed from head to toe in yellow
Petals and grape buds, rigid bark and dust-streaked
Patterns of summer, she lives naked among the hedges
And bordered paths of the garden. She hardly
Has boundaries there, so definite is her place.

Sometimes the golden flesh of the butterfly,
Quiet and needled in the spot of sun on her shoulder,
Can be seen and sometimes the wide blue wing
Of her raised hand before the maple and sometimes
The criss-crossed thicket, honeysuckle and fireweed,
Of her face. As she poses perfectly, her legs apart,
Some people can find the gentian-smooth meadow-skin showing
Through the distant hickory groves painted up her thighs
And the warm white windows of open sky appearing
Among the rose blossoms and vines of her breasts.

Shadow upon tattooed shadow upon real shadow,
She is there in the petaled skin of the iris
And the actual violet scents overlapping
At the bend of her arm, beneath and beyond
The initial act announcing the stems
Of the afternoon leaved and spread
In spires of green along her ribs, the bronze
Lizard basking at her navel.

Some call her searched-for presence the being
Of being, the essential garden of the garden.
And some call the continuing postulation
Of her location the only underlying structure,
The single form of flux, the final proof
And presence of crafted synonymy.
And whether the shadows of the sweetgum branches
Above her shift in the breeze across her breasts
Or whether she herself sways slightly
Beneath the still star-shaped leaves of the quiet
Forest overhead or whether the sweetgum shadows
Tattooed on her torso swell and linger
As the branches above are stirred by her breath,
The images possessed by the seekers are one
And the same when they know them as such.

And in the dark of late evening,
Isn't it beautiful the way they watch for her
To turn slowly, displaying the constellations
Penned in light among the black leaves
And blossoms of her back, the North Star
In its only coordinates shining at the base
Of her neck, the way they study the first glowing
Rim of the moon rising by its own shape
From the silvered curve of her brilliant hip?

Index of Authors and Poem Titles

Acknowledgments

~ *The Farm,* by Fred Chappell, reprinted with permission of author. *Delta Rain,* by Lily Peter, reprinted with permission of author's estate. *Starting a Pasture,* by Walter McDonald, reprinted with permission from University of North Texas Press. *Silver,* by A. R. Ammons, reprinted with permission of W. W. Norton. *Topsoil,* by Robert Morgan, reprinted with permission of author. *The Current,* by Wendell Berry, reprinted with persmission of Farrar, Straus & Giroux.

~ *A Country Life,* by Randall Jarrell, reprinted with permission from Farrar, Straus & Giroux. *Harvest,* by Henry Taylor, reprinted with permission of author. *Mississippi Mornings,* by Tom Dent, reprinted with permission of author's estate. *Shelter,* by Jesse Stuart, reprinted with permission of the Jesse Stuart Foundation. *Heritage,* by James Still, reprinted with permission of author's estate.

~ *Reaper,* by R. T. Smith, reprinted with permission of author. *Hanging Burley,* by Jim Wayne Miller, reprinted with permission of the authors estate. *Tobacco Days,* by Shelby Stephenson, reprinted with permission of author. *The Farmer,* by Ellen Bryant Voigt, reprinted with permission of author and W. W. Norton. *The Mullins Farm,* by R. H. W. Dillard, reprinted with permission of author.

~ *Dry Lightning,* by Marion Montgomery, reprinted with permission of author. *Because He Turned His Back,* by Edsel Ford, reprinted with permission of Wareagle Fair. *Delta Farmer in a Wet Summer,* by James Whitehead, reprinted with permission of author. *Kentucky Mountain Farm,* by Robert Penn Warren, reprinted with permission of William Morris Agency on behalf of author. *Steep,* by Robert Morgan, reprinted with permission of author. *Landlocked, Fallen, Unsung,* by C. D. Wright, reprinted with permission of author.

~ *The Migrants,* by Wendell Berry, reprinted with permission of author. *Deserted Farm,* by Guy Owen, reprinted with permission of Dorothy Owen and John F. Blair, Publisher. T*enantry (Polk County, Tennessee),* by George Scarbrough, reprinted with permission of author. *Old Rice-Fields,* by Edith L. Fraser, reprinted with permission of author's estate. *By the Fifth Generation,* by Ahmos Zu-Bolton II, reprinted with permission of author.

 ∾ *Crisis,* by Thad Stem, Jr., reprinted with permission of author's estate. *Scarecrow,* by William Sprunt, reprinted with permission of St. Andrews College Press. *Appalachian Landscape,* by John Beecher, reprinted with permission of Barbara Beecher. *Sonnet: An Old Fashioned Devil,* by Donald Justice, reprinted with permission of author. *A Pastoral of the Primitives,* by John Finlay, reprinted with permission of author's estate.

 ∾ *The Monday Before Thanksgiving,* by Thomas Rabbitt, reprinted with permission of author. *Kudzu,* by James Dickey, reprinted with permission from Wesleyan University Press. *Somewhere Along the Way,* by Henry Taylor, reprinted with permission of author. *Snapshot in the Red Fields,* by Jeanie Thompson, reprinted with permission of author. *My Grandfather's Funeral,* by James Applewhite, reprinted with permission of author.

 ∾ *Sweetbread and Wine,* by James Seay, reprinted with permission of author. *Conrad in Twilight,* by John Crowe Ransom, reprinted with permission of Random House, Inc. *My Father's Curse,* by Guy Owen, reprinted with permission of Dorothy Owen. *The Gardener,* by Rick Lott, reprinted with permission of author. *Laying By,* by Horace Randall Williams, reprinted with permission of author.

 ∾ *Gardening,* by John Allison, reprinted with permission of author. *Sunday Keeping,* by Robert Morgan, reprinted with permission of author. *The Terrapin Maker,* by Wade Hall, reprinted with permission of author. *Wise Enough,* by Edwin Godsey, reprinted with permission of author's estate. *Jonquils,* by James Applewhite, reprinted with permission of author.

ᕦ *Morning Glory,* by Richard Jackson, reprinted with permission of author. *Blue Hosanna,* by Sallie Nixon, reprinted with permission of author. *A Theory of Pole Beans,* by Nikki Giovanni, reprinted with permission of author. *December Portrait,* by David Daniel, reprinted with permission of Cumberland Poetry Review. *Another Valentine,* by Deborah Pope, reprinted with permission of author.

ᕦ *Granny Dean,* by Alvin Aubert, reprinted with permission of author. *Embroidery,* by Sally Buckner, reprinted with permission of author. *Farm Wife,* by Ellen Bryant Voigt, reprinted with permission of author and Wesleyan University Press. *Lineage,* by Margaret Walker, reprinted with permission from University of Georgia Press. *The Mountain Woman,* by DuBose Heyward, reprinted with permission of author's estate.

ᕦ *My Grandmother Washes Her Feet,* by Fred Chappell, reprinted with permission of author. *Planting in Tuscaloosa,* by Emily Hiestand, reprinted with permission of author. *At Jo's Funeral,* by Robert Gibbons. *He Makes a House Call,* by John Stone, reprinted with permission of author. *Before Tulips,* by Coppie Green, reprinted with permission of author.

ᕦ *Take Me Down That Row One More Time, Green-Eyed Boy,* by Bonnie Roberts, reprinted with permission of author. *Summer Food,* by Coleman Barks, reprinted with permission of author. *Putting up Damson Preserves,* by Becky Gould Gibson, reprinted with permission of author. *Full of the Moon,* by Robert Morgan, reprinted with permission of author. *Collards,* by James Applewhite, reprinted with permission of author. *Farmer's Market,* by Marcia Camp, reprinted with permission of author.

ᕦ *Picking Tomatoes on Sand Mountain,* by Anne George, reprinted with permission of author's estate. *Storm in the Briar Patch,* by James Applewhite, reprinted with permission of author. *Squashes,* by Charles Edward Eaton, reprinted with permission of author. *The Onion,* by Margaret Gibson, reprinted with permission of author and permission from Louisisana State University Press. *Riddle in the Garden,* by Robert Penn Warren, reprinted with permission of William Morris Agency, on behalf of author. *Going for Peaches,* Fredericksburg, Texas, by Naomi Shihab Nye, reprinted with permission of author.

∾ *Peaches,* by Catharine Savage Brosman, reprinted with permission from Louisiana State University Press. *Preserves,* by Jack Butler, reprinted with permission of author. *Meditation for a Pickle Suite,* by R. H. W. Dillard, reprinted with permission of author. *Root Cellar,* by George Scarbrough, reprinted with permission of author. *Volunteer,* by Robert Morgan, reprinted with permission of author. *The Flower-Hunter in the Fields,* by Jonathan Williams, reprinted with permission of author.

∾ *Buick,* by Andrew Glaze, reprinted with permission from NewSouth Books. *A Garden in Kentucky,* by Jane Gentry, reprinted with permission of author. *Going Home,* by Carol Prejean Zippert, reprinted with permission from NewSouth Books. *Making Our Garden,* by Emily Hiestand, reprinted with permission of author. *Dirt,* by Rodney Jones, reprinted with permission of author. *Primer on Digging,* by Dannye Romine, reprinted with permission of author.

∾ *Compost: An Ode,* by Andrew Hudgins, reprinted with permission from Houghton Miffin Company. *Buildings and Grounds,* by Henry Taylor, reprinted with permission of author. *Politics,* by Miller Williams, reprinted with permission of author. *Lazy Gardener,* by Helen F. Blackshear, reprinted with permission from NewSouth Books. *The Mower,* by George Garrett, reprinted with permission of author. *Letting the Garden Go,* by James Mersmann, reprinted with permission from NewSouth Books.

∾ *In the Yard, Late Summer,* by Dave Smith, reprinted with permission of author. *Crepe Myrtle,* by Charles Edward Eaton, reprinted with permission of author. *Late Summer,* by John Gould Fletcher, reprinted with permission from author's estate. *A Sort of Adagio,* by Sandra Agricola, reprinted with permission of author. *The Garden,* by

Fred Chappell, reprinted with permission of author. *After Gardening,* by Patricia Hooper, reprinted with permission of author. *A Charleston Garden,* by Henry Bellamann, reprinted with permission of author.

~ *Gift,* by Gerald Barrax, reprinted with permission of author. *Preservation of Life,* by Jennifer Horne, reprinted with permission of author. *Basil,* by Gibbons Ruark, reprinted with permission of author. *The Sadness of Gardens,* by Peter Huggins, reprinted with permission of author. *Cleaning the Shed,* by Catharine Savage Brosman, reprinted with permission from Louisiana State University Press. *Transplanted,* by Loretta Cobb, reprinted with permission of author. *Finding the Tattoed Lady in the Garden,* by Pattiann Rogers, reprinted with permission of author.

WORKING THE DIRT